STORIES FROM THE POTTER'S WHEEL

# PERFECTLY
# BROKEN

## DR. DENNIS SEMPEBWA

Publishing services by Evangelista Media & Consulting

ISBN: 978-1-0952448-0-7
ISBN eBook: 978-1-7327572-5-7

For Worldwide Distribution, Printed in the USA

1 2 3 4 5 6 / 22 21 20 19

# Dedication

This book is dedicated to the brave pilgrims and heroes of our faith who have gone before us. May their stories continue to echo through the generations.

# Acknowledgments

To my spiritual sons and daughters at The Father's Table. Thank you for agreeing to pen your stories. I am honored to call you family.

To Chelsea Pifer and Irina Schinkelshoek for helping me transcribe these touching stories.

Special thanks to Jeanne Cameron, Barbara King, Nathalie Sollberger, Dean and Lisa Romesburg, Gary and Angeli Valenciano, Jacques and Rachel Phelps, Pastor Frank Hernandez, and Pastor David Ndembe.

To our production team at EMC Italy for the excellent workmanship you bring to all our products.

To Lisa Romesburg for your dedication and service to the work of the ministry.

# Contents

# Introduction

I am privileged to lead a special group of spiritual sons and daughters from fourteen countries called The Father's Table. We are all ministers—pastors, homemakers, artists, businesspeople, executives, machine operators, designers, stylists, and so on from all walks of life. We are connected via a social media platform that serves as our virtual community. At The Father's Table, we encourage and challenge one another, share testimonies and prayer requests, and most importantly, we sharpen one another. In other words, we do life together.

One day, the Lord instructed us to share our stories. None of us would have anticipated what happened next. For a number of weeks, we opened our lives to each other and shared the gift of vulnerability. Tears ran down our faces as we attempted to walk in each other's shoes. The impact of that powerful experience resulted in this book.

Throughout the history of the church, God has used stories to touch the hearts of people worldwide. These stories filled the early church, centuries before the Bible was compiled or scholars created popular Christian theology. Everyday Christians shared personal stories of life-changing encounters with Christ.

The fact is: there is no greater pulpit than our stories. The Father's Table is populated by ex-addicts, ex-womanizers, ex-convicts, ex-manipulators, ex-haters—ex-sinners. We have all been broken in some way. Paul writes, *"For everyone has sinned; we all fall short of God's glorious standard"* (Romans 3:23). That's right. We have messed up, but guess what the next verse says, *"Yet God, in his grace, freely makes us right in his sight"* (Romans 3:24a). This means that God helps us hit the RESET button and calls us new. Paul goes on to explain, *"He did this through Christ Jesus when he freed us from the penalty for our sins"* (Romans 3:24b). Isn't that incredible?

Now here is the most exciting part of all. The work doesn't stop at the place of meeting with Jesus. In fact, that is where it starts. He takes our stories and uses them to draw others. So as you read these stories, allow God to speak to you about your own story. Perhaps it can encourage someone else to follow Jesus or to trust Him more.

Remember this—your story is a manifestation of the redemptive power of God. It tells of the power of Christ's finished work on the cross two thousand years ago. Don't be ashamed of it. Share it, write it, and sing it to the glory of God. It is God's story!

# Chapter 1

# Frank
## California, USA

*My old self has been crucified with Christ. It is no longer I who live, but Christ lives in me. So I live in this earthly body by trusting in the Son of God, who loved me and gave himself for me* (Galatians 2:20).

I was born in Southern California to a single mother. My biological father was involved in gangs and drugs and spent years in and out of prison. My grandfather didn't want him around, so I ended up being raised by my mom, grandparents, and aunts and uncles, all on my mom's side. I wasn't even named after my dad. I have my mom's last name.

I was about one and a half years old when my mom got involved with my stepdad. She got pregnant right away and the family started growing quickly. Both of my parents worked, so until I was school age, they couldn't really take care of me. My grandparents ended up raising me until the age of eight. I still went home on many weekends, though.

Growing up with my stepdad was pretty bad. I noticed he treated me different from my other brothers. He was also physically and verbally abusive. He beat my mom badly and also cheated on her.

One day my mom and I went to a local convenience store, up the street from where we lived. The store clerks knew me because we were regulars. On this particular day, my mom waited in the car while I went inside to buy milk. As I went to check out, I noticed a guy standing behind me, looking at me. Even though I was only eight years old at the time, I sensed something was wrong. As I put the milk on the counter, the man said to me, "Hey man, is that all you want? Don't you want some candy or ice cream or something? Pick something out and I'll buy it for you." The store clerk said, "Frankie, go outside and get your mom."

I ran outside, and the man followed me. He came up behind me and I saw my mom's face turn as white as a ghost. I asked, "Mom, who's this?" Before she could answer, the man said, "Hey, I'm your uncle, your mom's brother." He started talking to me and then told my mom, "Hey, I'm going to take him inside to buy him something." So, I went inside and started looking at the candy. He said, "Go ahead and get what you want." I remember saying, "I'm not really allowed to have candy." My brothers were allowed to have candy, but I wasn't.

After he bought the candy for me, I asked him, "How come I don't know you? How come I've never met you?" He said, "I'm your mom's brother and your dad doesn't like me. You can't tell him you saw me." As he was talking to me, he kind of bent down on a knee and looked into my eyes as he spoke. No one had ever done that to me before, and it made me feel like there was something different about him.

A couple of weeks later, I woke in the middle of the night with a bad stomach and chest pains. My grandmother woke and asked me what was wrong. I told her I didn't know what was going on, but that my heart hurt. I felt really sad, and I couldn't sleep. A couple of days later, I went to visit my other grandmother, my stepdad's mom. She said to me, "You know that guy you like, your uncle? Well, he's not really your uncle. He's your dad and they just killed him." Then she walked away without saying anything else or making any attempt to comfort me.

I was blown away. Everything hit me at once and, in that moment, everything finally made sense. I knew why I was treated differently from my brothers. I cried and cried. I was so angry and hurt. I was especially angry at my stepdad for never allowing me to see my father. I started asking questions like, "Who am I? Who is my family? What am I?" I felt rage come over me. All I could think was, *I want to kill him...the man who killed my dad...I want to kill him.* All I could feel was hate. I was only eight years old. I remember crying, my fists clinched, swinging at the air in anger. I remember thinking, *Now I have to learn to kill.* Most kids grow up wanting to be superheroes, police officers, or football players—but I grew up wanting to kill.

As time passed, my mom and stepdad bought their first house. They moved several miles away from the barrio in Corona to an upper-middle class, mostly white neighborhood. I moved back in with them and things were better for a while. Still, I often thought about my dad's death and my deep desire to avenge him. I remember thinking, *I have to figure out how I'm going to do this.* I thought, *I have to start learning how to be a gangster...how to act like them, talk like them, and walk like them. I have to learn how to work my way up in the gang to know how to do this thing.* Throughout those years, it was always in the back of my mind. I often thought about how to kill the person who killed my dad.

When I was only twelve years old, I joined a gang in my old neighborhood. Late at night, I would climb out my window and hike four miles to the hangout. I started doing drugs, and before I knew it I was already too far gone to pull back. My mom found out when I got pulled over and arrested for being under the influence of PCP.

That began years of me going in and out of the correctional system. God didn't allow me to do too much crazy stuff though, because I was often busted and incarcerated. But when I was out, I ran a hard-core muck, so to speak. I was always fighting and doing stupid stuff with my gang. I ended up missing all of my high school years. Every time I was put into a placement home, I was kicked out because they would say I was too gang affiliated, so they'd send me back to juvenile hall.

I got out of the gang lifestyle for a little while when I was fourteen years old. That's when I accepted the Lord. My mom said I was being tossed all over the room as if a demon was throwing me, until the pastor prayed for me. It was a pretty crazy thing I went through.

After that, I told the guys in my gang, "I have to get out of the gang because I'm a Christian now." They told me, "This is what you have to do—you have to walk the line." That meant that the whole gang would form two parallel lines and I would have to walk between them while they beat me. I agreed and, as I walked down the line, I could see them hitting and kicking me, but I didn't have a single bruise or scratch.

I went to my aunt's house afterward and she asked, "What happened? Did you get out of the gang?" She saw I looked fine, so she didn't believe that they had beaten me. I said, "Tía, they made me walk the line, but nothing happened to me!" The gang was so mad because they were trying to make an example of me, but God supernaturally protected me.

But I still didn't learn. I backslid and got back into a gang.

After years of going in and out of juvenile hall, I was released for the final time when I was seventeen, during what would have been my senior year of high school. A couple of months later, I met the woman who would eventually become my wife. We became good friends and I fell deeply in love with her. I had been getting strung out on heroin and knew I had to kick the habit if I wanted to be with her. I also knew I needed to leave the gang. I told the guys I was ready to leave. They weren't happy about it and there was a lot of back and forth discussion. It took almost six months, but eventually they let me go.

My mom and stepdad were getting a divorce, so my wife and I moved in together. We started partying together, getting high together. I had traded heroin for speed. It was a big mess. We finally came to the Lord in 1996, but once again, we backslid four years later. I started hanging out with some gang members again and got involved with some really bad guys.

I really messed up my life again and brought my family down with me. The police raided our home and I was arrested. I was bailed out and went on the run from the police. I was eventually caught at a motel and went to prison for a couple of years. In prison is where He found me. I turned my life over to the Lord and have been serving God ever since.

When I was paroled, I got a job as a drafter even though I had no experience. I worked my way up into management and now I'm the Safety and Fleet Manager at my company. I'm also ordained and serve as the senior pastor of our church. I've been traveling with Dr. Dennis and his team. God is really moving in our lives. We're seeing tremendous things happen. God is using my wife and me to touch so many lives in our community and our area.

My name is Frank Hernandez, and I am perfectly broken.

# Chapter 2

# Barbara
## Illinois, USA

*The LORD is my strength and shield. I trust him with all my heart. He helps me, and my heart is filled with joy. I burst out in songs of thanksgiving* (Psalms 28:7).

My father abused me physically, emotionally, and sexually from the age of six until I was fourteen. I was raised in the Lutheran Church and remember the first time I heard the Christmas story of Jesus. I was around five years of age, attending a children's class, and something inside of me got excited. I believed it and I wanted it. That I knew. But religion, not relationship with Jesus, is what I was taught. My conversations with Him were not prayers, but more like begging. I thought that God must have made a mistake and left me here. I wanted to go to Heaven to live with Him.

I lived most of my childhood petrified with fear of my dad. Normally, I hid in my room reading a Bible—until one day my dad got angry and took it away. Tired of waiting on God to take me home to Heaven, at about eight years old, I tried to commit suicide. I rarely slept, so my mom told the doctor and they prescribed a mild sedative to help me sleep even though it was highly unusual to medicate kids my age.

One night after praying, or rather begging Jesus, I couldn't take it anymore and decided to take my own life. I swallowed as many pills as I could and laid down on my bed with my hands clasped. I felt almost a sigh of relief that it would soon be over and I would be with Jesus. To this day, I can still feel it vividly, the separation of spirit and body. But I felt trapped in the body. I couldn't get out. That was the only time I ever heard God's voice audibly. He said, "You will not die, but live for Me." I argued a little with Him in my spirit and said, "Don't tell me I can't die too."

Then He told me to get up and drink a cup of water. It was as if He had asked me to lift up the house. The room was spinning. I crawled to the bathroom down the hall, took a little paper cup, and drank some water. To this day, I can still remember that was the best cold water I had ever tasted. As soon as I drank it, I vomited. The next thing I remember, I woke up still hovered over the toilet seat. I was extremely sick and weak, but to stay home from school would mean torture from my dad. So, I quietly made it out the door where one of the girls, Tammy, saw me and helped. I told her what I had done, and she stayed by my side all day at school. I still thank God for Tammy.

One day, I found my sister crying. I knew Dad was molesting her. I promised her I would find a way to stop the madness. So, I ran away twice to my extended family. That way Dad would focus on me instead of them. "The next time you run away," he warned, "I will slice your throat." No one lifted a finger to help me. They were too afraid of Dad.

I ran away a third time; and this time connected with an old grammar school friend who was affiliated with a gang. We lived on the streets, slept in empty buildings, and ran the streets. I lived this way for about three months. Then, one day we made a plan to go to California together, so we could start new lives. That same day, my oldest brother and his friends found me.

During my time living on the streets, I met a young man in the gang. After my family found me, he wanted to get out of the gang, go work with his dad, and straighten out his life so he would be good enough to marry me. If you know anything about gangs in Chicago, you know that's just not possible. Once you pledge allegiance to the gang, you don't get out alive. Somehow though, they let him go; but unfortunately, his sister got caught up in the same gang. One night, he went to try and get her out, but they turned on him, called him a traitor, and shot him dead in the chest. The family didn't allow any of us to go to his funeral.

When my brother found me, my dad's history of abuse was revealed, and he went to prison. At that time, a child the age of fourteen was not allowed to testify in court. But they gave special permission for me.

During the trial, his lawyer came at me. She said that I seduced him and that I, at six years old, was a whore. I was distraught. I remember sitting in the backseat of the car, driving home from court that day. I was conversing with God silently, telling Him, "My mom's going to kill me." She had already said, "If this isn't true, I will kill you for having put everybody through this." If something didn't happen to change the outcome of the trial, I would be dead.

During that conversation with God, I remembered the black trunk. I blurted out, "He keeps a black trunk in his bedroom!" "What?" my mom and brother asked. Again, I said, "There's a black trunk in his bedroom!" He kept it locked and no one, not even my mom, could go in there. So, I said, "It's in the trunk!" I knew the evidence we needed was in there. My mom, brother, and I went straight to it when we got home. We broke off the lock and that is where we found all of the diaries and pictures of all that he had done. He wrote explicit details, even including the times he tried to kill me. We also found out that he had another name, wife, and children somewhere else.

We went back to court. The judge took the evidence, but to protect me he did not read in open court. When the trial resumed, he said to the court, "I had to stop reading. I couldn't finish reading the diaries and couldn't look at any more of the pictures." He counted at least ten times my dad tried to kill me. That was it. The case was over, and my dad ended up going to prison. His psychological evaluation labeled him a psychopath. That meant he was capable of slicing my throat, and then turning around and having an ice cream cone, thinking nothing of it.

Shockingly, most of the family and my mom rejected me because of the verdict. To them, I ruined their lives. We didn't know anybody from his side of the family, but suddenly his sister showed up and bailed him out. We had an order of protection against him. He started stalking me, and one day he showed up in front of my work in violation of the order. The police came and put him back in prison.

Years later, I got married, but could not get pregnant due to the sexual abuse. I had severe endometriosis and went through a number of surgeries. After I finally conceived, I tragically lost the baby due to an ectopic pregnancy. I was rushed into emergency surgery that lasted over six hours.

My husband was consumed by his own pain. He didn't know why this had to happen to him, why he couldn't have children. He left the hospital and never came back to see me. My inability to have a baby eventually fractured our marriage. My religious upbringing had taught me that a woman who couldn't bear children for her husband was worthless and a shame to God. He decided to divorce me, which further alienated me from my family who believed it was a sin.

I had nowhere to live, so my brother took me in against the objections of his wife. For years, I was tormented mentally and emotionally. I kept working hard even though I never slept. I lost a lot of weight and began to spiral downward really fast. I felt like I wanted to die again.

One night as I cried that I couldn't take it anymore, I heard an inner voice counteracting all of the other voices screaming in my head. This one was softer and simply said, "Ask Jesus. Call out to Jesus and He will deliver you." I argued and said, "No, I'm such a shame. How could I even face God with all that I have done?" But the voice kept saying softly, "Ask Jesus. Call out to Jesus."

Finally, I cried out and said, "Jesus, if it's true, and there is anything You can do with my life, then it's Yours. I have nothing left. Do whatever You want. Just stop this!" That is the last thing I remember until I woke up the next morning. I had not slept that much since the divorce. I was totally changed. The voices in my head were gone. Inside, I felt complete peace, quiet, and joy. I even felt a sense of happiness. I went to work and during my lunch break, I went to the park and began to read the Bible. Except this time it spoke to me and I felt like it had a voice. I began reading in the book of 1 Corinthians, and to this day it's my favorite book.

From there, my life took an about-face. I soared at work and church, growing and learning all I could. Years later, I had to have a laparoscopy to examine me internally. "I read everything more than once, and know what the doctors did," said the doctor, "I would swear in any court that you never had endometriosis. There is not a single piece of evidence of it ever being there." That meant there was no reason I could not get pregnant. Jesus had healed me.

Even though I never had any biological children, God gave me the opportunity to mother a Russian orphan, whom I could not adopt for many complicated reasons, who still calls me "Mom." My then-husband and I also adopted a Romanian son whom I love dearly.

My journey led me to serve with Dr. Dennis and his wife, Ingrid, in various capacities. We launched a church together 2008. I served as his administrator for Eagle's Wings International (EWI), and as a professor at our college, Eagle's Wings Bible Institute. Today, I am a marketing director at a mechanical company and I own my home.

God has done a great work within and around me. With everything that He's peeled away from me and changed within me, knowing what I know now, I wouldn't change a thing. Even though I was desperate at times, I learned to have faith in God, to walk with Him, and to trust Him with everything. Instead of looking to people, even though He uses people to do His bidding, I learned to trust God. I also needed to be cleansed of religion and the bad experiences I had from toxic churches. I know better now.

Today, I focus on the true Word of God and feel so free from religion. I have learned to be so thankful in my life. I purpose to live thankfully. I believe these are the keys to life—to always live thankfully, to always invite God into your day, and to ask Him to help you. I don't go a day without doing this. There were so many times I should have been dead and yet He delivered me every time.

My name is Barbara King, and I am perfectly broken.

# Chapter 3

# Steven
## Kampala, Uganda

*Search me, O God, and know my heart; test me and know my anxious thoughts. Point out anything in me that offends you, and lead me along the path of everlasting life* (Psalms 139:23-24).

I was born into a polygamist family in 1964. In our part of the world, polygamy was the norm. My mother was only the age of nineteen and my father was already thirty-nine years of age. She was no match to the co-wives, so the marriage did not last. When I was six, my parents divorced. Around the same time, I also lost a sister from a chocking accident at the dinner table. The rest of my siblings and I went to stay with my mother. But because culture dictated that children grow up in the father's house, we were all dragged back to my dad's place.

That started a life of hardship and terror. My father had fifteen kids by four different wives, living in multiple houses. There were so many of us kids, but we stayed at home with one mother at a time. There was never enough—not enough beds, food, or the various other things we needed as children.

We were not poor. In fact, we were quite wealthy by the standards of the community where we lived. But that didn't translate into our home. My father was oblivious to what was happening in his own home. My mother would ask my cousin to sneak us out of the home to get some decent food to eat. Those years toughened me, but also traumatized me. In hindsight, I deeply resented my father. He was a typical workaholic, always gone, and unaware of our desperate need for a father.

I wasn't very rowdy and naughty, but I was dragged around by peer pressure by my schoolmates and siblings. We did all of the things that boys do. I was prone to that. It was kind of fun. But, at the same time, it was also difficult. That season would significantly impact who I am today.

My small stature made me susceptible to bullies. I grew up thinking, *I never want that to happen to me or to my child, or to any child for that matter.* In school, my academic performance was average.

In my early teens, I crossed paths with a boy at school who used to preach the gospel under a tree. A bunch of us guys ganged up on him and really made his life difficult, or so we thought. We would ask him all kinds of questions. Surprisingly, he had answers for every question, which both angered and mesmerized us. Eridard was unstoppable. One day, he grabbed the attention of a whole bunch of us in the middle of the morning, and we all snuck out to go to church. It was 1981, and the nation was experiencing a revival, church doors were always open. We all got saved that week. From that day, I have never looked back.

It was a fun time. Churches were on fire with daily services. That was new to us because we grew up as committed Episcopalians. My dad had donated benches to our local Anglican church, and engraved our names on them. I was christened and raised in strict Anglican tradition, through and through. Thus, it was really hard for my father to come to terms with daily church services. In the morning, I would go from home to school and back to church from school, which meant that I didn't get home until late at night. This infuriated him, but I was so sold-out that I didn't care. He hardly had any time for us anyway.

I started walking with Christ. I met so many people and made so many friends. A couple of years later, I met Dr. Dennis for the first time. I remember this one time when we were at church. Someone had brought instruments, a big upright piano and a guitar. I was taken with the guitar and had a friend of ours patiently show me some chords. Dr. Dennis went for the piano. I saw him play his first note on a piano. To see what the Lord has done with that talent is amazing.

Eventually, my mother also joined the church. By this time, she had remarried. Unfortunately, my stepfather was killed, which made her a widow with seven kids at an early age.

Shortly after, I joined a Baptist church and that opened a whole new arena for me. We used to have Bible studies, practice Scripture memorization, participate in small groups, sing and dance, and attend retreats and lock-ins. I had so much fun and these things really resonated with me. I concentrated on attending the Baptist church more than the Pentecostal churches.

Later on, God opened a door for me to work in England, and later in the United States of America (USA). While in the USA, I worked at an automobile dealership in Denver, Colorado, which was most eye-opening. I would later return to school, at Colorado Christian University. Four years into my stay, in 1996, I decided it was time to return home.

Less than a year after I returned to Uganda, my mother passed away due to kidney failure. She was the pillar in my life. I was devastated, and my life took a turn. I was left to care for seven kids, most of them teenagers. Around the same time, I met a great girl named Angela. We worked together at a tech company and were later married in 1999. Angela would combine her paychecks with mine so that we could take care of my siblings. They are all doing well today, and I thank God for that.

We had our first child a year after our wedding. Seven years later, God gave us a second child, and, a third child thirteen months later.

My work life has included working with the Southern Baptist Mission in Uganda and multiple telecommunications companies. I also worked for the Samaritan's Purse organization. In fact, one of the highlights of my life is having breakfast with Reverend Franklin Graham when he visited Uganda, and flying with him to the field on a very old DC3 plane that the ministry owned.

Eventually, Angela and I decided it was time to set up our own work. We started a semi-charity school called BBEL Academy, which I now run full-time. Our dream is that we take children into kindergarten or elementary school and walk alongside them through to adult life.

We are blessed to serve in a small church in the city suburb in the marrieds ministry. But I also have the huge privilege to serve with the EWI team whenever they are in the country. I set everything aside and serve God that way. I am so thankful for friends and family.

I am thankful to God for bringing me thus far. I have gone through ups and downs. Where I am right now, it is only God who has brought me here.

My name is Steven Muyimbwa, and I am perfectly broken.

# Chapter 4

# Donna
## Rancho Santa Margarita, USA

*Trust in the LORD with all your heart and lean not on your own understanding* (Proverbs 3:5 NIV).

I was born and raised in California. Ours was a home filled with extreme fear. My father was very militaristic, while mom, on the other hand, was very passive. Hardly any subject was ever addressed. We lived under a strict code of silence, with barely any social interconnectedness. Dad was verbally abusive. He knew how to make us feel very insignificant. My older siblings were treated worse than me. He would physically abuse them without any remorse. My life was terrifying. Unfortunately, it seemed like Mom was helpless, often crippled with fear herself.

By the time my oldest sister turned eighteen, she already had two kids. She asked me to babysit them, with strict instructions not to tell Mom. You can imagine how that compounded my fears, especially since I was only nine years old. One night she came home with a man. They were both very drunk. After she passed out, he came to my room, drugged and sexually molested me at knifepoint. The incident crushed me and emotionally shut me down. I never told anybody. And why would I? We never really talked about things like that.

I became a robotic thirteen-year-old who had chosen to simply go through the motions, almost unable to really feel anything. Then came the boys…and then the severe panic attacks, to the extent where I was afraid to leave home, a condition called agoraphobia. I was in a constant state of crippling panic. I could not even walk to school. Things would go blurry.

At age twenty-five, I got married. We were both emotional cripples. He had no idea how to be a husband; and me, I didn't know how to give or receive love. About a year and a half into our marriage, we called it quits. I was a wreck. For the next three years, I was in and out of inpatient psychological care facilities. No, I was not addicted to drugs or alcohol. My wound was debilitating fear. The programs seemed to help as long as I was in the facilities, but the moment I entered the regular world, I would regress.

Eventually, I found the Lord. When I heard the clear message of the cross, I was hooked. Jesus is the only One who made sense to me. When I worshipped Him, I felt alive. He made me feel loved and accepted for who I was. Since first believing, He has helped center me. I am determined to live the life He has called me to live, and determined to believe what He says about me in His Word—that I am cherished, beautiful, and loved as His child, and that no matter what anybody did to me, I am safe in Him. He has persuaded me concerning this truth, "Donna, anything and everything that ever happened to you has nothing to do with you, it had to do with their shortcomings. You forgive them and keep walking forward."

I am Donna Farley, and I am perfectly broken.

# Chapter 5

# Gary
## Manila, Philippines

*Trust in the Lord completely, and do not rely on your own opinions. With all your heart rely on him to guide you, and he will lead you in every decision you make. Become intimate with him in whatever you do, and he will lead you wherever you go. Don't think for a moment that you know it all* (Proverbs 3:5-7a TPT).

I come from a family of seven siblings. It's the beginning years of my journey that marked me the most. For years, we all lived under the same roof. My mom and dad always left our doors open for friends to come and hang out with family members. Never was there a day that music wasn't played. To say that my childhood was joyful would be a gross understatement. Yes, we had our fair share of family issues, but the fun times far outweighed the heavy times.

My world crashed when I learned that Mom and Dad were getting a divorce. Then came the unimaginable—our house had to be sold! My siblings and I would be separated. My thirteen-year-old mind could not process how two seemingly loving people could part ways like that. Having grown up a stanch Catholic—even served as an altar boy—I was devastated. How could God allow this? How could He let our happy family suffer?

The next thing I know, my sisters and I were air-bound for the USA to live with my mother. It was one of the most painful things I had to endure. In my simple mind, that was "Strike ONE" for the Lord. He had let me down.

At fourteen years old, I was diagnosed with type 1 diabetes. Three years earlier, I remember seeing an eight-year-old niece screaming and running away from her nursemaid as she chased her with a syringe. My uncle told me she had diabetes, and it was time to take her shot. *Wow, that's one thing I hope I never get,* I thought. So my grim diagnosis was "Strike TWO" for the Lord. He had let me down once again. Slowly I felt resentment starting to build up in me toward Him as I couldn't understand why all these bad things were happening. I felt that maybe it was punishment for past mistakes.

After a year in Florida, I returned to the Philippines. I was elected rector of my high school. After one busy weekend filled with activities, Dad surprisingly came to see me. I still remember his bright yellow shirt. He was quiet, almost absent as I shared testimonies from my busy weekend. Suddenly, he stopped me, held me by the shoulders, and said, "Son, the house burned down last night." Here was my dad trying to recover from deep loses and now the house is gone? That was "Strike THREE." As the baseball metaphor goes, after three strikes, you are out.

How could a good God be so mean? *That's it, Lord,* I thought. *I can't trust You. I am done with You. I am on my own now. Don't call me...I will call You if I ever need You!* I couldn't see how any of this made sense. My broken life seemed to be completely pointless. Yet, like a beautiful mosaic, God was at work. God was charting the pathway that I have walked to get to where I am now.

Check this out: Had I been home during that fire, I doubt I would've been around today as it started in the middle of the hallway and my room was located at the end of it. There would've been no way to escape the flames. So, thank God for life, but that's not all. When my schoolmates' parents heard about the incident, they raised funds for me to attend college.

After the fire, I moved into my sister's house with just the clothes on my back. She had an antique piano which, though out of tune, became my escape and provided me a way to learn how to write songs. God also blessed me with a voice that to this day has touched millions around the world—multitudes who have wrestled with life the way I have. Countless lives have been moved to trust God with their stories.

We were told by my doctors that a type 1 diabetic is usually given about a thirty-year life span from the day of diagnosis. I was diagnosed at fourteen years of age. At the time of this writing, I am fifty-four years old. I am a walking, living miracle of God's healing hand. I have been able to travel the world to share Jesus with people. He has blessed me with a wonderful wife, Angeli, and three magnificent children.

Has God answered all my questions? No. Yet this one thing is clear—God does work ALL things for the good of those who love Him and are called according to His purpose. Although I face different and new issues today, I am confident that the Lord isn't done with me just yet.

My name is Gary Valenciano, and I am perfectly broken.

# Chapter 6

# Irina
## Thun, Switzerland

*And don't be intimidated by those who are older than you; simply be the example they need to see by being faithful and true in all that you do. Speak the truth and live a life of purity and authentic love as you remain strong in your faith*
(1 Timothy 4:12 TPT).

I was born and raised in Switzerland in a Christian family with three older brothers. My childhood was very safe and filled with lots of good memories. Dad is a doctor and Mom a homemaker. Even though he worked so many hours, Dad managed to keep his work from encroaching upon his responsibilities at home. I remember our Wednesday daddy-daughter times when we'd both stay home to spend time together. I learned to stand up for myself, growing up with three brothers, whom I adored. School was great too—good friends, good grades…overall a healthy family environment.

Mom and Dad welcomed all kinds of people into our home. Friends would hang out in our home almost all the time. Every so often, we'd even help house people who had fallen on hard times. I absolutely enjoyed that—loving people back to health. It was always nice to share with others the peace of God that was in our family.

I vividly remember this one incident that happened while I was in sixth grade. Out of nowhere, my best friends abandoned me over a misunderstanding. I never told anyone about it. I am not sure they would have thought anything of it. My brothers were out being boys. Suddenly, I was alone. Just then, I was drawn to the only safe place

I knew—to God! I learned to trust Him. I made time for Him, and started hearing His voice.

I remember one time laying in my backyard, asking God if I'd ever have my friends back. Just then, I looked up to the clouds and saw a YES! Excitedly, I went to school the next day, fully trusting God to keep His promise. Well, nothing happened...for three years. The isolation brought me closer to my church family. I developed friendships that I still enjoy today.

During that time, one of my high school teachers taught a philosophy class that really tested my faith. In the final exam was a question challenging the notion that miracles authenticated God's existence. Knowing how my atheist teacher wanted me to respond, I chose to defend the thesis. Unbeknown to me, something began to change. I started to believe in relativism. My values became blurry. I began to overcompensate; trying to prove that Christianity was fun. I started drinking and making out with guys I would never even date.

Right after high school, a door opened for me to enroll in Youth With a Mission's Discipleship Training School in Hawaii. God used that time to clean me up and dismantle lies I had believed about myself. I redirected my focus and found my identity apart from friends, family, giftings, and stuff. God saw the girl inside and set me upon a wild journey.

After I returned, I joined a movement in my town called Open-House4Cities. It was there that I met my husband, Jan. Together, we would grow in our faith as we did life with a group of radical, passionate young people. A boldness came over us as God removed the fear of people from us. We prayed for the sick and shared our experiences with the lost. It seemed as though we loved Jesus more each day. I saw people being changed by the love of God. I was also involved in leadership at my church, leading youth and serving on worship teams. That's when I met Dr. Dennis and the EWI team. He invited us to journey with him, which took my passion to a whole new level. I married my handsome Jan and soon after we embarked upon a wild adventure of fun and ministry together.

My passion is to see people touched and transformed by God's power.

My name is Irina Schinkelshoek, and I am perfectly broken.

# Chapter 7

# Jan
## Bern, Switzerland

*My heart spills over with thanks to God for the way he continually empowers me, and to our Lord Jesus, the Anointed One, who found me trustworthy and who authorized me to be his partner in this ministry* (1 Timothy 1:12 TPT).

I spent a big chunk of my childhood in Bosnia, a country in Southeastern Europe. With loving missionary parents in a great Christian home, mine was a perfect Christian upbringing. My dad was a significant role model for me. He seemed to always do the right things.

We generally got along very well as a family. But even in the midst of that, my curious heart was being pulled to compromise. I felt drawn to the forbidden. Young as I was, barely eight years old, I'd stay out late, I'd lie to my parents, steal money from Mom, and get into all kinds of trouble.

At age nine, we moved back to my birth country of Switzerland. The reentry was very rough for me. I had never really lived in a Western culture. I struggled to make friends. I also grappled with school. I was a jokester, which caused classroom disruptions. The school administration became concerned about my mental health and decided to put me through a barrage of tests. I hated doing homework with Mom. We got into a lot of fights as I struggled to focus and concentrate. I began to think that I was stupid.

My relationship with my parents suffered. I started to pull back and share less of what was really going on inside me. I always believed in God; but for me, Christianity was boring. It seemed like all the fun was out there: snowboarding, drinking, skating, biking, and so on. So I went for it.

I started drinking alcohol and watching pornography. Dad had always told me that porn would destroy my future marriage, which terrified me. I felt like I was living two lives—the worldly life that on the outside seemed to make me happy, and the "good kid" life around church as a son of a national Christian leader. I hated that I wasn't authentic. I wished I could talk to Dad, but I knew he'd be disappointed in me. I felt like a total failure.

My heart broke when Dr. Dennis came to our home and prophesied over me: "You don't have to be like your dad. God has a plan for your life and desires to use you greatly." Those words literally jolted me. It took me some time to actually believe it; but when I did, God began to create a new identity inside me. That weekend was a turning point for me. I decided to stop watching porn, which broke the habit. That same weekend, I began to seriously date Irina, who would become my wife. God really set me free.

Since then, I have served with my dad's ministry, OpenHouse4Cities, and also frequently travel on global missions with EWI. The God-life has become real and exciting. I didn't just hear about what God is able to do, I have seen it and experienced it. God can use me and work through me even though I thought I was useless for His Kingdom. I'm excited to see what He has in store for me.

My name is Jan Schinkelshoek, and I am perfectly broken.

# Chapter 8

# Rachel
## California, USA

*So be strong and courageous! Do not be afraid and do not panic before them. For the LORD your God will personally go ahead of you. He will neither fail you nor abandon you* (Deuteronomy 31:6).

I was raised in a somewhat volatile neighborhood. By age five, I had been sexually molested by two men and a woman. After several other incidents, I started to think this abuse was normal. But as I hit my teens, I started realizing my broken mindset, and feelings of guilt and shame started to torment me. I felt dirty and ugly.

When I turned twelve, my aunt Lucy started taking me to church. I remember singing songs about Jesus. As I cried myself to sleep at night, I would question God, "Why did You allow all that hurt to happen to me?" Gradually, He began to speak comfort to me.

Unfortunately, as I turned thirteen years old, I slipped away into drugs to numb the pain. At age seventeen, I became a young unwed mother to a precious daughter named Michelle. Unfortunately, she passed away at two years old in a car accident. At the time, Anita, my second daughter, was only five weeks old. Once again, I questioned God. My life became a messed-up bundle of pain, so deeper into drugs I went. I got married briefly, and God gave me another daughter, Regina. Once again, that marriage collapsed, which plummeted me further into drugs.

I got into another relationship, and became pregnant again. My boyfriend persuaded me to abort. I even set up the appointment with the abortion clinic, but God intervened through a customer at the grocery store where I worked. She insisted I visit her counseling agency after I inadvertently shared my predicament. It was God's providence that saved my son. Carrying Andrew helped heal the deep wounds that I had carried from the loss of my first daughter. I had been pummeled by feelings of inadequacy and guilt. I felt like a bad mother, never being enough.

God would lead me back to Him. I got baptized and eventually married my son's dad. Bad mistake. He was a philanderer, so that marriage collapsed. Straight away, I jumped into another serious relationship and got married again. Another bad mistake. Before long, I was stuck in a cold marriage to an unfaithful husband. My life was like a train wreck. I fell away from the Lord and for fourteen years, lived a prodigal life.

God reconnected me to a high school crush named Jacques. We were both recovering from terrible marriages. He used our love to heal and restore us. We got married and what a journey it has been!

Today, we serve with our pastor and old friend, Pastor Frank. God has lit a fire inside of me. I'm so excited about what God is doing in my life. It feels like the Lord has taken me back to my early days of innocence when I first knew Him.

My name is Rachel Phelps, and I am perfectly broken!

# Chapter 9

# Jacques
## California, USA

*He's the hope that holds me and the Stronghold to shelter me, the only God for me and my great confidence* (Psalms 91:2 TPT).

I grew up in a home filled with domestic violence. My mom and dad used to drink a lot of alcohol and would constantly fight. I remember seeing Mom being beaten severely by my father. She even tried to commit suicide a few times. Almost every other night, I would plead with the neighbors to call the cops in the wee hours of the night. Sometimes I'd hide under the bed, literally petrified. One day, Dad put a gun to his head and told me to pull the trigger. I missed, triggering yet another visit from the cops.

Although Dad made good money, we seemed to be broke all the time. Often, Mom would send us to beg for food or money from our neighbors. But seeing that we were the "neighbors from hell," they'd understandably avoid us. I felt so poor when I saw kids playing with toys or eating candy. We couldn't afford any of that.

One day, I decided to improvise. I started asking neighbors if I could mow their yards or run errands for them. At eight years old, I started working. Every weekend, I would clean apartments with a kind old lady named Peggy, who had become my night nanny whenever the police came to my house. Sometimes, I would sleep on her sofa. I learned to earn my keep. I also got to afford some of the common luxuries like going to the cinema.

Unfortunately, my turbulent childhood predisposed me to a life of violence, gangs, and addiction. By age eleven, I was smoking pot.

At thirteen, I started running around with gangs. By fourteen, I was smoking PCP, a narcotic. My eldest brother protected me from so much, including Dad's physical abuse. Unfortunately, I'd lose him to a drug overdose in 1986. The loss devastated me. My brother after him was a major drug dealer, which exposed me to a whole other life I never knew existed. I ran to drugs and gangs. Violence and addiction became my lot.

At age fourteen, I got an after-school job in a body shop. We painted airplanes, cars, school busses. I learned how to be a mechanic. Eventually, the late work hours broke me; I couldn't concentrate in school, until someone mentioned night school. I immediately applied and made a critical change in my life for the better. I increased my work hours to full time during the day and took classes in the evening.

By eighteen, I was tired of it all. I had tried to get into professional sports (baseball), but my drinking disqualified me. Just then, someone told me that I'd start playing better if I used meth and cocaine. So I did. So there I was, playing ball in tournaments throughout California, Nevada, and Mexico while totally strung out on drugs.

At twenty-four, I got married and we became pregnant. All I thought about was our child. I even passed up an opportunity to work as a NASCAR mechanic on their racing team. I had worked in the pits with them at the Riverside Raceway when they came to town. I thought fathering would change me. Well it didn't. Instead, the drug abuse got worse. My frustrated wife became verbally and physically abusive to me. I tried to change, even returning to baseball.

In January 1991, my friend invited me to watch a football game. All night we played games, did drugs, played pool, and partied the night away. At about 4 a.m., my friend announced to us that he had just found his wife in bed with another man. "I don't what to hear your problems," I said. "I have enough of my own. What you need to do is give your life to the Lord!"

Just then, a voice spoke to me saying, "No. You need to get right with Me right now!" I was immediately sober. Was it the drugs playing tricks on me? I tried to drink another beer, but it tasted bitter. I was freaking out, so I decided to go home. The next morning, I woke up sobbing. "Lord, I'm tired of this," I pleaded, "Forgive me of my sins. I promise to serve You for the rest of the days of my life."

Since that day, January 14, 1991, I've been serving the Lord through countless trials and tribulations. It has been the most incredible adventure.

My name is Jacques Phelps, and I am perfectly broken!

# Chapter 10

# James
## Port Harcourt, Nigeria

*That the God of our Lord Jesus Christ, the Father of glory,*
*may give to you the spirit of wisdom and revelation in the*
*knowledge of Him* (Ephesians 1:17 NKJV).

My father's name was Nathan Wosu-Wachuku. He was married to three wives including my mum, Mercy, who was from the Ibo tribe. We are from the Ikwerre tribe of Rivers State in Nigeria. As far as I can recall, my father always hated my mother because of her passion for God's Word and the divine wisdom she was gifted with by God.

School came easy for me, but my father wouldn't send me. I would cry to my mama, begging to be sent to school. She didn't have any money, so she decided to reach out to friends and neighbors for loans to send me to school. We were very poor. Mom literally financed my school this way until I graduated from university. I remember selling textbooks to classmates to make some extra money to support myself.

I joined the National Service, our mandatory military service, right after graduation. Upon my return home in 1986, I learned that my father was very sick. With my meager resources, I hospitalized him so he could receive medical care. I didn't mind that he had refused to send me to school. I helped him as unto the Lord. My father passed away later that year. With my new job at the Nigerian National Petroleum Corporation, I was able to help with the costly funeral arrangements. Shortly thereafter, I relocated to Lagos to work in the banking sector where I immediately enjoyed good success as the Lord favored me. I was on my way to the top.

In 1992, my promising career was interrupted by the Lord when He called me into the ministry. I had an encounter with the Lord Jesus Christ when I was in my room alone and He gently reminded me of His goodness to me throughout the years. I served under my father in faith, Apostle Zilly Aggrey of the Royal House of Grace International Church in Port Harcourt. During that time, the Lord connected me to my mentor, Dr. Dennis Sempebwa.

Today, I am honored to serve as director of missions for our churches across the nation. My job is to travel through the backside of our nation planting churches in rural communities.

My name is James O. Chuku, and I am perfectly broken.

# Chapter 11

# Michelle
## Illinois, USA

*All Scripture is inspired by God and is useful to teach us what is true and to make us realize what is wrong in our lives. It corrects us when we are wrong and teaches us to do what is right. God uses it to prepare and equip his people to do every good work* (2 Timothy 3:16-17).

I grew up in Chicago, hailing from first-generation, Italian-American parents, both high-school dropouts. By twenty-four years of age, my mother had four children. I was the youngest. This was my family: violent, loud, argumentative, and chaotic.

When I turned eleven, Mom told us she was pregnant again. Naturally, we were thrilled, until we noticed Mom's desperate sobs. Next thing I remember is Dad explaining to us that we had another sister from another woman. I was devastated. My bubble had burst. I became angry.

Mom decided to forgive Dad's infidelity. They blended the family adding my stepsister to the household, making ours a very full house.

A fiery preacher from West Virginia came by the house and prophesied to me concerning God's purposes in my life. I was only twelve years old. I felt the Holy Spirit falling on me and gave my life to the Lord.

My teen years were turbulent. Nobody was discipling me; I just kind of bounced around, angry at Dad, still trying to coexist with the chaos in our home. So I decided to lash back. I decided to become a hairdresser, party, and live life to the fullest. That is when I met my first husband, at nineteen years old. We were clones of my mom and dad; two passionate people madly in love with each other, constantly fighting. It's all I knew—you fight, say mean things, you forgive.

At twenty-three, I was pregnant. So we rushed to City Hall, got married, and had our son. My pregnancy was filled with stress, turmoil, and suicidal thoughts. When my son Dino was born, he was given a 1 percent chance of survival. As they prepared to fly him away for emergency care, a verse came to my mind: *"Where two or three are gathered together in My name, I am there in the midst of them"* (Matthew 18:20 NKJV). God miraculously healed him to the amazement of the medical community. Our marriage collapsed after fifteen months. I had found my own place, so I decided to work hard to grow my hairdressing business and fight to survive. It's all I knew to do.

As Dino turned six, I met a man who was the complete opposite of my first husband—very reserved and quiet. I thought we'd be perfect because he was nothing like me. He also had full custody of his two kids. We got married, had two more kids together and for years, I was perfectly happy raising our family, until the 2008 recession hit. We lost our home and pretty much hit bottom.

As I struggled to make sense of the losses, I found God in the fog. After a time of fasting and prayer, I began to write my story. Soon after I was done, a friend introduced me to Dr. Dennis, who helped me get it published. I wasn't looking for fame or notoriety. Since its release, not my book, BUT GOD, has touched countless people I would have never possibly reached.

As financial pressure mounted, the scales fell off my eyes. The Lord began to show me my husband's underhandedness. Although he had treated me better than any other man, the lies and manipulation caused our marriage to fissure. One day, he just up and moved out of state with his kids. The pain of betrayal was unbearable. In all, even still, I learned to rest in God's providence and grace. I learned to hold on to Romans 8:28 which says how our God works all things together for the good of those who love Him and have been called according to His purpose.

This is the message the Lord has put on my heart to share with the nations: Christ is our true hope. When money, family, health, or status is lost, He is always there as the true anchor for your soul.

Am I out of the wilderness yet? No, but I am trusting that my hope and my faith in God are going to work ALL things out for my good.

My name is Michelle Fatigato, and I am perfectly broken.

# Chapter 12

# Mary
## Illinois, USA

*We are hard pressed on every side, but not crushed; perplexed, but not in despair; persecuted, but not abandoned; struck down, but not destroyed* (2 Corinthians 4:8-9 NIV).

I was born two months early. Consequently, I had many health problems, including epilepsy. Because of the medications, I struggled to wake up and would often wet my bed.

My childhood was full of turmoil. I endured a lot of physical and emotional abuse. I remember having hot, dry red pepper in my mouth to stop me from crying. Many nights, I was awakened by beatings.

My father had nicknames for everybody. He liked to call me "Big Dummy," "Klutz," and "Beëlzebub," which means "Prince of Darkness." My father dabbled in the occult and frequently practiced witchcraft. He didn't believe in the Holocaust or the moon landing. He was paranoid; recording people's private conversations. So my friends stayed away from our home.

School was rough. I had learning disabilities, which were exacerbated by the medications that knocked me out during class. By the time I was in high school, my family had moved thirteen times. Consequently, I was unable to keep up academically and socially.

I became a Christian when I was nine years of age. Not long after, I was miraculously healed of epilepsy. Even still, my choices were not always the best. While in college, I fell for a young man who skipped town right after I became pregnant with a daughter I named Katie.

Shortly thereafter, I met Anthony, who loved me in spite of the fact that I was a single mother.

One day, Anthony came home with an FBI subpoena. Confused, I ran to my dad who persuaded me to immediately divorce him, abort my six-month pregnancy, and move in with them. I did, only to find out that Dad was trying to take custody of Katie just before she was born. They had pressured me into giving them custody of her.

Anthony and I got back together and God blessed us with another daughter, Rachel. She brought such joy into our lives, even though it was rather short-lived. I plummeted into a deep depression, which led to several suicide attempts and multiple hospitalizations. Years of abuse and guilt had taken their toll. I felt like I had nothing to offer Anthony.

We were locked in a punishing three-year custody battle for Katie. Anthony wasn't allowed to see Katie because my parents falsely accused him of being connected to the mafia. They insisted that I have supervised visits with Katie due to my history of depression and hospitalizations. I still feel sad when I remember sitting in busy shopping malls with Katie, on Christmas and Easter, watching her open gifts from me.

The custody battle drained us financially, emotionally, and physically. We went through hours and hours of psychological testing. Even our IQ scores were taken into account to determine our ability to parent Katie. My parents used things I wrote in my personal journals to build a case against me. I felt so hurt and betrayed. We dealt with corruption and went through a number of attorneys because my father manipulated and bribed them. He also brought Katie's biological father into the court battles.

We were preparing for a jury trial when my attorney told me I had to stop taking antidepressants. The medication levels were never quite right and that made it difficult for me to recall details and answer questions in court. Miraculously, that was the last time I ever took them. At the same time, Katie's biological father was reassigned to Germany, so he was unable to appear in court. At that point, my father began to realize he was going to lose the case.

Even though she was still living with my parents, I often picked up Katie from school. On her eighth birthday, I was especially excited to see her.

I waited outside her school, but she never came out. I found out that she had not been at school for three days. Dishearteningly, the principal had not notified the court-appointed lawyer. We called the same FBI agent who had questioned my husband years earlier and he became involved in our case, now at the federal level. We found out that my dad planned Katie's abduction. Somehow, he managed to have my daughter board a flight to Germany using a boy's name to join her biological father. I remember my attorney's chilling words, "You may never see your daughter again."

I prayed, "God, I don't want to see my daughter torn between my parents and me anymore. Please stop this. Just stop it. No more..." I remember going to church the next Sunday. The pastor called Anthony and me up to the front. The pastor then asked everyone to come up and stand behind us, to storm the gates of hell, and to pray and take authority over the situation.

The next day we went to emergency court. The judge read through all of the court documents and decided to intervene directly. My father returned to Florida with Katie, and immediately sought out more attorneys to build a new case. That also backfired. As soon as they entered the courthouse to present his phony case, an agent grabbed Katie, and my parents were arrested, but my father bribed his way out of jail the next day.

God continued to provide for us.

A year later, my dad passed away. He had asked to see Katie and me, but couldn't. I remember his lifeless body. He looked like he had been in a concentration camp. It took ten years to get back into a relationship with my mom and twelve years for my sister and I to reconnect. There are parts of our relationship that we will never get back, but I'm very grateful to God for what we have.

We thank God every single day, and often, for all that He has done. We experienced the cost of choosing the Lord over my family. Looking back, the choice was never really a choice, because I was always drawn toward the Lord.

My name is Mary Fatigato, and I am perfectly broken.

# Chapter 13

# Nathalie
## Thun, Switzerland

*Before I formed you in the womb I knew you; Before you were born I sanctified you; I ordained you a prophet to the nations* (Jeremiah 1:5 NKJV).

I was born into a Christian family in Switzerland. My parents already had two sons—my brothers—when they had me. They were so happy to have a girl. Being the youngest and the only girl made me feel very special. I felt like a princess. That lasted for three years and then something happened. Although my parents did not desire any more children, my mother became pregnant and it was another girl.

Something happened to me when she was born. It was like a door opened for a lot of lies and false thinking to come into my life. I began to think, *I'm not special. I'm second. I'm not really loved...*a lot of bad thoughts about myself.

School was hard for me. It was so hard for me to learn. Often the teachers would say to me, "You are no good." I didn't think they liked me at all. This formed the basis for the internal narrative I started to believe about myself: *You are not enough.* This lie became part of my identity. Even though I loved Jesus a lot, I did not believe in myself.

I started thinking about going to school to study education. I have always loved children. In fact, my biggest dream was to become a teacher; but again, I didn't think I'd be any good at that either. Consequently, I only completed a two-year certification and got a job at a toy store. Although I sold toys, I didn't really work with the children.

I worked there for six years. Yes, six lonely, unhappy years. I knew and loved Jesus, but I had a lot of toxic thinking. My greatest desire was to meet a guy, get married, have children, and build a family.

One day as I was walking home from work, I became overwhelmed with grief. "If You are really there, if You really hear me, if You really love me, then come on!" I cried out to God. "Come on and speak to me and say You love me and give me a bigger picture of my life. I need to know what I am doing here. God, please, give me a sign that You are really there."

That was my cry that Saturday. On Monday, I went to work having forgotten about my prayer. While there, a woman came into the store. I had met her before, although I didn't know her well. She walked over to me and said, "Jesus sent me to you. He says, 'You are important. I know you. I see you. I see your heart's wish. And, I will give you a lot of gifts in the coming years. I will meet you.'" My heart was so touched. Yes... Jesus knew me. I was glad that He knew me.

God started to speak to me about me. He healed my heart and started to correct my way of thinking. He opened a door for me to join OpenHouse4Cities, a community of passionate young people who are radically in love with Jesus. I began to grow as God started to show me all this stuff that He had put inside me. I began to believe that He thought well of me.

Something else was also happening. For years, I had been feeling really empty inside. I still had the dream to have a husband and family, but Jesus was speaking to me that He is enough for me. I met Him in a new way. I remember going to our prayer room and laying it all down before Him, saying, "Hey, Jesus, I give all of my dreams, all of my wishes, and all of my heart—I give them to You." A new relationship began. I learned the love of Jesus in me. It was so different.

We all need so much freedom, love, and peace in our hearts, and in our bodies. Unfortunately, we search for this in people, in relationships, or in other things that come from the outside. God showed me that His love can really fill us. It is so different because it comes from the inside out. Because I finally understood He lives in me and loves me, all of my thinking began to change. I thought, *Whoa, He is really in love with me!*

It was so different. I began to walk in a new way, in a new identity—my identity as God's beloved child. He began to speak truth to my heart, to tell me that He is so proud of me and that He is enough for me.

Today, I can truly say that Jesus is really enough. I feel so much love in my heart, in my mind, and in my body. I have a new identity. I can stand before people and talk to them. That doesn't terrify me anymore. The reason it is so different is because this big, beautiful God loves me. It's not really important what people think about me. I can talk to them and tell them that the love of God is so much more than we can find in any relationship, hobby, or anything else. We won't find a love like His anywhere else.

I'm so excited about what is coming. I am His child and I have His freedom in my heart and I walk in it. I wish all of this for every person I meet, whether married or single, young or old, educated or not, homeless or wealthy. None of that matters. Only Jesus matters. He seeks to be your King, your Beloved, and for His freedom to reign in your heart. That is all we need and it is the best thing.

My name is Nathalie Sollberger, and I am perfectly broken.

# Chapter 14

# Susanne
## California, USA

*Your word I have hidden in my heart, That I might not sin against You* (Psalms 119:11 NKJV).

One of my earliest memories was a dream I had when I was five years of age. It's a dream that has brought comfort to me as I weathered some of the roughest storms of my life. I remember the grey and white backdrop. I was sitting in His lap, with His arms around me and my head on His chest. I knew it was Him—Jesus! I still remember it like it was last night.

I was born and raised a few miles from Disneyland. My pentecostal parents raised me, my sister, and brother in church. Dad was a hot-tempered pastor of Grace Chapel in Orange. Ever since I can remember, I was not wanted by either of my parents. I was verbally and physically abused; slaps, switches, belt, you name it! Mom always told me that she couldn't wait for me to grow up and leave. Many nights I would hear them comparing me to others as they shamelessly asserted that I would never amount to anything.

I was very fortunate to attend a Christian school from kindergarten to third grade where music was introduced to me. From then on, it was as though music was looking for me. I was routinely given solos and was involved in choirs, drama, plays, community theatre, anything in the arts. Those experiences opened a pathway to the entertainment world and Hollywood. With all that going on in my life, I can't understand to this day why my dad never once let me sing in his church.

I still remember the daily three-mile hike to school. I remember being stalked by lewd men who kept volunteering to drive me. It's only by

God's grace that I was not raped or molested. I would often hear an angel whispering in my ear, "Susu, go hide!" God was showing me His love.

One day, a twenty-one-year old man named John came into our family. All of sudden, Dad promoted him to head deacon. Right away, he seemed to be more important to Dad than any of us. Out of the blue, Dad proposed that I marry John. I violently protested, but Dad threatened to disown me. After months of emotional manipulation, he wore me out. I married John, but the marriage didn't last even a year.

Shortly after the divorce, John introduced me to his gay partner, and in a subsequent family meeting, he delivered a bombshell announcement that my dad was gay too. My family was crushed, especially me. I felt betrayed. I had just had a baby son. Dad had been living a double life. My forced marriage to John was a sham, intended to cover their love affair. Dad had cheated on Mom for most of their marriage with many men he met in gay bars.

We also learned that Dad had AIDS. Imagine the shame of having the preacher's family being tested for HIV. Dad died a terrible death in 1996. To protect my mom from embarrassment, we told everyone that Dad had died from complications resulting from a botched blood transfusion. To this day, my siblings want nothing to do with church.

Since the church had rejected me, I sought visibility in the entertainment industry where I felt understood and accepted. But even as I mingled with big shots and dove deep into the world, I knew God had a purpose for me. God would bring me a wonderful man, Dana, who loved me well. Dana was being drawn by Jesus. He wanted to go to church, but I resisted. In 1999, we both surrendered our lives back to Jesus.

We immediately dove in, serving on worship teams, growing in the faith. We formed a group called BETH, which provided us an avenue to serve Jesus Christ. The Lord has allowed us to lead thousands of believers in true worship.

Jesus gets sweeter and sweeter every day. Look how far He has brought us. For us, this is way more than music, singing, writing and playing songs, or leading through worship. It's dwelling in Jesus's presence. It's the Father's love and His Holy Word that keeps us glued together.

I have learned not to place my eyes on people, but to only focus on the Lord. Every day, I am learning more about the unrelenting love of my heavenly Father, Abba Daddy, who is unlike my struggling, broken earthly dad.

My name is Susanne Elston, and I am perfectly broken.

# Chapter 15

# Dana
## California, USA

*"For My thoughts are not your thoughts, Nor are your ways My ways," says the Lord. "For as the heavens are higher than the earth, So are My ways higher than your ways, And My thoughts than your thoughts. For as the rain comes down, and the snow from heaven, And do not return there, But water the earth, And make it bring forth and bud, That it may give seed to the sower And bread to the eater, So shall My word be that goes forth from My mouth; It shall not return to Me void, But it shall accomplish what I please, And it shall prosper in the thing for which I sent it"* (Isaiah 55:8-11 NKJV).

I grew up in the Los Angeles area of California. I took to music early in life. I remember going to Hollywood a lot, playing in a lot of clubs, doing a lot of stupid things, drugs and alcohol and all that stuff. Initially, we did a lot of copy songs, then we started writing our own music and doing original songs. Eventually, we caught a break and started playing in some better clubs in Hollywood doing our own original material. Word got to us that Warner Brothers was considering signing us to record our songs. As exciting as it was, that deal fell through. In hindsight, God knew what was best for us. That path was going to lead me to untold dark places.

Soon after that, I stopped playing music, got married, and settled down. For a while, I was away from it all. During the hiatus, all my equipment was stolen. Next thing I know, I get a call from the police asking me to come get it. Apparently, the thief had passed away and the police found it. I went down to the station, procured it, and brought it all back home. I remember kissing my guitar and saying, "I'm never gonna put you away again." I started playing music again, and our marriage collapsed.

Shortly thereafter, I met Susanne. She joined our newly formed R&B band, and we started making music together. As word spread around Los Angeles about our band, I met Jesus in 1999. We formed a Christian band and joined the worship team at the church. That long journey has led us here.

Has the road been smooth? Not at all. We have been attacked, betrayed, and misused. Yet we love the Lord even more. Today, we minister in a lot of different churches across Southern California.

My name is Dana Elston, and I am perfectly broken.

# Chapter 16

# Judith
## Mengo, Uganda

*I can do all this through him who gives me strength*
(Philippians 4:13 NIV).

I was born at home in the 1980s with a neighbor as the designated midwife. I contracted tetanus from the unsterilized equipment and was rushed to one of the main hospitals in town. By the time I was admitted, my organs had started shutting down. Half of my body was not functioning, so they placed me in a ward that housed babies who had died. For six months, I was barely hanging on to life; my precious mother was by my side. I was fed intravenously and given countless injections, which had all kinds of side effects. I was told years later that a group of missionaries prayed for me and that God miraculously sustained me from week to week. The doctors said I would never conceive because of the trauma to my newborn body, but God has given me two beautiful children.

Homelife was turbulent. My parents fought all the time. Dad was an alcoholic. Poverty, loneliness, and strife was the order of the day. They would separate by the time I turned four years of age. Mom immigrated to Denmark, and I was left with my dad and stepmother who raised me.

When I was a teen, Mom decided to fly me to Denmark to move in with her. I was naturally excited. I was a budding teenager looking for identity and love. Unfortunately, I found the opposite. For reasons best known to her, Mom did not like me. She hated that I loved my dad. I felt that way because he had taken care of me and not abandoned me; he had taken me to school and made sure there was always food on the table. But she reminded me of how much she had sacrificed for me; how because of me, she was stuck in a ward with dead babies for six months, and how I had caused her to contract ulcers because of it.

Things came to a head between Mom and I, so I moved out of her house, turned my life over to the lordship of Jesus Christ, and started serving God. I loved church and church people. I loved helping people. Everything was rosy until someone, a believer, betrayed me. I didn't know that church people behaved that way. I was brutally attacked and almost fell away from the Lord because of it. Although I clung on to the Lord and refused to go back into the world, I was bruised. My self-esteem took a hit, as insecurity gripped me.

Thank God I stayed the course. I married a minister who invited me to serve alongside of him to build our church. We have been blessed with two beautiful babies. I lead our women's ministry and am currently pursuing a Master's degree in African studies.

I have come to know that God loves us all and cares about all of our brokenness. He is restoring my happiness and He is using me in various ways. He has infused me with boldness and strength.

I am Judith Yusuf, and I am perfectly broken.

# Chapter 17

# June
## Texas, USA

*I can do all things through Christ who strengthens me*
(Philippians 4:13 NKJV).

I grew up in western New York State right outside of Buffalo. I had loving parents, five older sisters, and an older brother.

I don't remember many things about my upbringing, but a few stand out. I remember child services wanting to take me away from my family when one of my sisters who was supposed to be home to watch me wasn't. I was only eight years old. I also remember military police officers coming to my house because someone had stolen checks that belonged to my brother-in-law who was in the army.

The next thing I remember was being lonely—spending days at home with my brother. All my sisters had left the house and were married. Our parents were busy working. My brother took advantage of the isolation and started beating and molesting me. I was only ten years old. That went on for two years until my father found out. My parents decided I should not be left alone with my brother after school. I was to stay with my sister at her house until they got home.

That seemed to work out well until one Friday evening when I had returned home to do my chores. My brother started to come at me so I went to kick him in the stomach, but instead hit him in the groin. Unfortunately for me, the molestation did not stop until he started dating after which my parents and I moved to Cincinnati, Ohio. From there, we moved to Texas where I finished high school.

Through all of this I knew that God was watching over me. Indeed, I've always believed in Jesus. I started teaching Sunday school in 1983 and taught until 1985. This whole time I thought that I had truly accepted Jesus in my being. That did not actually happen until I was attending a revival in 1995. There, I actually felt the need to let Him have complete access to my whole being and have been growing in His grace ever since.

My name is June Whorton, and I am perfectly broken.

# Chapter 18

# Derric
## Texas, USA

*"No weapon formed against you shall prosper, And every tongue which rises against you in judgment You shall condemn. This is the heritage of the servants of the Lord, And their righteousness is from Me," Says the Lord* (Isaiah 54:17 NKJV).

I was raised in a Church of Christ denomination and remained faithful to my patronage throughout my childhood. At nineteen years old, I walked away from church and God altogether after I was abused by one of the elders. Alcohol and drug abuse became my lot, losing everything.

About that time, I met June. I was twenty-five years old. June was tough on me. She told me she would not date anyone who abused drugs. So I had to quit. I asked Jesus to come into my life. He told me, "Derric, you are done with this!" We were married and have been doing life together for thirty years.

In 1995, we joined the First Baptist Church in Hempstead where we have served in various roles and ministries through the years.

In 2009, I had a huge wake-up call. The Lord had been urging me to slow down. Not listening, I kept up the pace, thinking, *Lord, if I don't keep going, who will do all the work?* In April, my body sent me a stronger message. After not feeling well for three days, I decided to have myself checked out by our doctor. To my shock, I was having a stroke—double arterial blood clots. Well, God definitely had my attention then. As I sat in recovery, He took me through the books of Job and Jonah. I made a full recovery and returned to work the following month with no repeat repercussions from the stroke, by God's grace.

After meeting Dr. Dennis and encountering God at the gatherings in Houston, we decided it was time to join the team to serve in the nations. I remember the day we landed in Belize, our first international mission trip. God really showed up that week.

My heart did act up again, but through prayers and our Father's healing hand, I am still here telling His story. Experts told me that both events should have been fatal—but God definitely has more for me to do here.

My name is Derric Whorton, and I am perfectly broken.

# Chapter 19

# Mandy
## Liverpool, UK

*Don't just pretend to love others. Really love them. Hate what is wrong. Hold tightly to what is good. Love each other with genuine affection, and take delight in honoring each other. Never be lazy, but work hard and serve the Lord enthusiastically. Rejoice in our confident hope. Be patient in trouble, and keep on praying. When God's people are in need, be ready to help them. Always be eager to practice hospitality* (Romans 12:9-13).

I live in Liverpool, Mersey side, in the United Kingdom. I grew up in a lovely home; and by every estimation, I had an awesome childhood, amazing in fact. Life was fun and filled with laughter.

At fifteen years of age, I was tragically raped and thus began the spiraling downward. For the next decade, abuse, domestic violence, alcohol, and drugs became part of my life. In the process, I had two beautiful children who are now teenagers.

One day, I stumbled upon a little leaflet asking, "Do you want to go to Africa to help kids with HIV/AIDS?" Right then, I signed up, even though I was still addicted to drugs and alcohol. In three months, I raised the 6000 pounds needed to fund the trip. I went to Kibera in Kenya, Tanzania, and Zanzibar, and I absolutely loved it. Three weeks into the mission trip, I gave my life to Christ, and was baptized in the Indian Ocean. The trip changed me.

I came home and told my whole family that I was now going to church, and that Jesus had saved my life. I had supernaturally come off the drugs and alcohol while I was in Africa and felt whole and healed.

I also started taking my kids to church. I would return to Africa in 2009. Eventually, my kids would also visit that great continent to do missions. God has really brought me out of the grave.

Today, I help addicts get into rehabilitation. We also feed the homeless and local families who are struggling. In all, we feed roughly five hundred people a week. God has been so gracious. He has used me in spite of my past, pain-filled life. It's an honor and a pleasure to serve these helpless, desperate people—and most importantly, to bring them God's Word.

My name is Mandy Upton, and I am perfectly broken.

# Chapter 20

# Sami
## Kampala, Uganda

*The Lord is my light and my salvation; Whom shall I fear?*
*The Lord is the strength of my life; Of whom shall I be*
*afraid?.... One thing I have desired of the Lord, That will*
*I seek: That I may dwell in the house of the Lord All the*
*days of my life, To behold the beauty of the Lord, And to*
*inquire in His temple* (Psalms 27:1,4 NKJV).

I've been a musician and performing artist since I was five years old.
My earlier influences came from my grandparents on my father's side,
who raised me.

At age six, I joined one of the big churches in Kampala, then called
Kampala Pentecostal Church. But it was in high school that I fully
committed my life to Jesus Christ. Right away, I started serving Jesus,
becoming a youth leader and working with the orphaned children's
choir called Watoto.

Watoto toured the United Kingdom and the USA. When that season
ended, I went back into leadership with our young people. Eventually, I
would move to another region where we started planting churches. In
2007, I stepped into pastoring, which led to several pastorate positions
in various churches around the country and beyond: youth pastoring,
worship pastoring, and now senior pastor of a worship ministry called
Praise City.

Meeting Dr. Dennis was one of the greatest blessings in my life.
Though I grew up watching his band Limit X and fell in love with
them, I had never really gotten close to him. When the opportunity

arose, we instantly became friends. I then followed his ministry and got to know him.

Today, I know him not just as a mentor, but also as a spiritual father. The impact of our relationship on my ministry and personal life has been phenomenal. Yes, I will keep serving Jesus here in Uganda. I will still make music and lead hungry folks into God's presence as a worship leader. I will train leaders and continue to do life with my beautiful daughters—Esther Shekinah who is thirteen, and Ramayah Precious who is eleven.

My name is Sami K, and I am perfectly broken.

# Chapter 21

# David
## Illinois, USA

*Is there any encouragement from belonging to Christ? Any comfort from his love? Any fellowship together in the Spirit? Are your hearts tender and compassionate? Then make me truly happy by agreeing wholeheartedly with each other, loving one another, and working together with one mind and purpose. Don't be selfish; don't try to impress others. Be humble, thinking of others as better than yourselves. Don't look out only for your own interests, but take an interest in others, too. You must have the same attitude that Christ Jesus had (Philippians 2:1-5).*

I was born in the Democratic Republic of Congo into a missionary family; number two of four children. As with most missionary families, we moved a lot—America, Europe, and parts of Africa. That was my life.

At thirteen years of age, I gave my life to the Lord. My dad often reminds me that I was a very rebellious kid, but when the Lord got a hold of me, my life changed drastically. During high school, we were based in Germany. I was enrolled in a missionary boarding school called Black Force Academy. There is where I made some of the biggest strides in my early spiritual development. Interestingly, I didn't really have a passion or desire to become involved in ministry. I wanted to serve outside, but not in church. I guess I'd seen too much dysfunction in church. I saw how Dad was hurt and mistreated by the people he served. I didn't want to do that.

Well, the opposite has happened. For the past twenty years, church is where I have poured my life, serving the Lord as a youth pastor and a worship pastor, and what a rewarding journey it has been!

Fourteen years ago I met my wife, Loma. She is a beautiful Ethiopian woman. God has faithfully blessed us with three wonderful children—Maisha, Joshua, and Joe. They love the Lord, they love to worship, they love people—and that was a prayer I had before they were born.

We're currently pastoring in Decatur, Illinois, about two hours south of Chicago, and the Lord has been faithful. I'm honored to be counted worthy of championing the cause of Christ around the world with incredible brothers and sisters who love the Lord and are hungry for more.

My name is David Ndembe, and I am perfectly broken.

# Chapter 22

# Dean
## California, USA

*No eye has seen, no ear has heard, and no mind has imagined what God has prepared for those who love him*
(1 Corinthians 2:9b).

I was born on August 9, 1959, to a divorced mother. I was called The Mistake Child because I was conceived during my parents' separation. I was always looked at and treated differently because I was a constant reminder of my father. My late older brother was Mom's pride and joy; and for some strange reason, up until the age of fourteen, she made me aware of it. As a teenager, I was pressured to find work to provide rent money for Mom. When I resisted, she threw me out on the streets—and to be honest, I was relieved.

I moved into a small hotel room in a beach community, and thus began my wild adventure. I started a lawnmowing business at the age of fifteen with a schoolmate who had a truck. We secured a large, two-year contract from the Irvine Corporation. We eventually sold our company to a developer and started a new construction cleanup business at twenty years of age.

Unfortunately, my business partner took all of our money and moved to Costa Rica with his girlfriend, leaving me holding a massive business debt. That was the first time I reached out to the Lord. Even though I didn't really know Him, I felt His abiding presence in my life. He helped me pick myself up and showed me a way out by investing into a third business.

The backstory of my life throughout my teenage years was punctuated by self-medication. I was surrounded by people who shared the similar pain of loneliness and despair. We all medicated by using drugs, alcohol, and promiscuity. I married and was blessed with a child, but I couldn't shake the destructive behavior. The marriage collapsed after three years.

Then I found a Southern Baptist Church where I connected with a mentor who led me to the Lord. I remarried and had two more children, but I was still masking my pain through drugs and living chaotically. After twelve years, my addictions ended that marriage as well, and my faith in God took a backseat. I rationalized my pain. I told myself that God understood my addictions.

I went back into construction and recommitted my life to the Lord. I was a California boy and my view on the type of woman I was supposed to be with was completely different from what the Lord brought me. When I met Lisa, she was at rock bottom. She was a drug addict stuck in an abusive relationship. By God's grace, He saw us through it all and broke the hold of drugs from both our lives. We grew together in the Lord in a very special way using a year-long, cross-country road trip. We got clean and developed a trust in Him like nothing we'd ever experienced.

God blessed me with a wife who has truly been my true soulmate. He has blessed our business, which has enabled us to minister to others throughout the world. Lisa and I share priceless memories of mission trips throughout Africa, Ukraine, and Mexico.

My name is Dean Romesburg, and I am perfectly broken.

# Chapter 23

# Cam
## Ramstein-Miesenbach, Germany

*For the LORD your God is living among you. He is a mighty savior. He will take delight in you with gladness. With his love, he will calm all your fears. He will rejoice over you with joyful songs* (Zephaniah 3:17).

I came to Christ at age 17. Joined the United States Air Force as a Security Forces Airman shortly after graduating from high school. Eight years later, I had completed five tours to Iraq, one in Africa, and one in Afghanistan. While there, I continued to attend base chapels regularly, volunteered to assist chaplains, and established Bible studies in squadrons on every deployment. Without a doubt, chaplains, lay ministers, and chapel communities played an integral part in my overall spiritual formation.

All of my deployments were to combat zones. I performed a broad range of duties, from flighting security for the Special Operations Chinook helicopters and C-130 airplanes bringing wounded operators, to personal security details for Air Force Office of Special Investigations (OSI) agents off-base. We trained police departments and responded to whatever calls we received. All of these life and death situations produced a real devotional lifestyle in me and solidified my spiritual disciplines and daily faith. I was honored to see many soldiers and airmen making decisions to follow Christ.

I remember losing a dear friend to a sniper on October 17, 2006. That previous Sunday, the two of us went to an Army Chapel that was set up in Saddam Hussein's old palace where Lee recommitted himself to the Lord, days before he died. He was 21 years old. I was emotionally devastated. Lee and I felt called into ministry and had plans to attend

Bible college. Clearly, the Lord had other plans. But that deployment augmented my call to chaplaincy.

My journey had helped me realize that I had an intense burden to reach the lost ones who were serving abroad. I had seen the physical, emotional, and spiritual toll that warfare tends to place on military members and their families, and how the Word of God could give them the hope they needed. I saw how the chaplains played a vital role in being literally the hands and feet of Jesus in combat zones, and they are the "boots on the ground." Sometimes, they were the only people that could be found for miles in places like Iraq and Afghanistan who were preaching the gospel.

After coming to this realization, my wife and I both sat down and decided to take some huge leaps of faith. In August of 2009, I separated from active duty, finished my bachelor's in pastoral studies by the end of 2010, and my M.Div. in 2013. I was planning on starting my Clinical Pastoral Education training when we received orders to go to the Misawa Air Base in Japan in 2014. For a while, it seemed like I was getting further from my calling to minister to United States Armed Forces service members. But nothing could be further from the truth.

Upon arriving in Japan, Chaplain Daniel Karanja introduced my wife and I to Ed and Faith Ferguson, a missionary couple who were the pastors of Neighborhood Church Misawa. The Fergusons would ask us to pastor Neighborhood Church Misawa, and on May 18, 2014, I was installed as lead pastor of that Assemblies of God fellowship.

Our time in Japan was one of the most fruitful experiences of my life. We had a great rapport with the Japanese locals and also with the other English-speaking pastors there. I had to do bi-vocational ministry, working full-time as a civil service employee on base in addition to pastoring Neighborhood Church Misawa. The church was very small, so the salary I received was not enough to live on. In spite of all that, the Lord grew our church from 6 people to over 100 every Sunday in a short time. We were honored to pastor Neighborhood Church Misawa from May 2014 until August of 2017, when we were shipped here to Ramstein Air Base in Germany.

In July 2018, I was commissioned as a Civil Air Patrol (CAP) Chaplain. At the time of this writing, I am interning at Landstuhl Regional Medical Center as a CAP Chaplain, so I'm able to don a uniform once again, without having to necessarily travel to a combat zone. My work here at Landstuhl Hospital is extremely rewarding. I am able to be on the flight line for incoming and outgoing patients. I have partnered with the Wounded Warrior Project on base. Every Wednesday, I have the privilege of leading a lunchtime Bible study, and to conduct daily prayers and collect prayer requests from a prayer room in the ICU.

I don't regret any of my experiences, and CAP has been a great opportunity for me. I am so excited to engage in discussions with other pastoral clinicians and medical chaplains and to continue to minster to the human spirit with the Institute of Clinical Pastoral Studies.

My name is Cam Swanson, and I am perfectly broken.

# Chapter 24

# Amie
## Riverside, California

*Guide me in your truth and teach me, for you are God my Savior, and my hope is in you all day long* (Psalms 25:5 NIV).

I grew up in Whittier, California. I never really knew my dad. I only met him once, and talked with him a few times. Mom only found out that she was pregnant with me after she ran away from him to escape his brutal physical abuse. She tried to end the pregnancy but was too far advanced for an abortion. At first, she drank, smoked, and did everything a pregnant woman is not supposed to do. After a couple of months, she changed her mind, and decided to have me. She was only nineteen years old when she had me. She said I was the best thing that ever happened to her. I was her second child by him. Shortly after I was born, she divorced Dad.

Mom single-handedly raised us but was in over her head. I started doing drugs at age eleven. By the time we hit our teen years, we were out of control, doing drugs, and running around in gangs. I remember losing my innocence at age fourteen.

At eighteen, I ended up in jail for driving under the influence of alcohol (DUI). My so-called friends claimed I had stolen their car so they could claim insurance money, and that sealed my conviction, which landed me in county jail. I knew I needed to make a change, so I moved out of Corona and checked myself into a women's home where I started to experience change. I decided to give my life to Jesus Christ.

Walking out in freedom was not as easy as I thought. As discouragement set in, I didn't know how to handle it. I didn't understand the process, so I got confused and started acting out. The following year,

I quit the program and left the home. Shortly thereafter, I met Manuel, my husband. He gave his life to the Lord when I took him to church for the first time.

We were in and out of church for a several years until the age of twenty-five when I decided to stop playing nice with God and really grab hold of Him. That is when He dramatically changed me. I knew then that my life was never going to be the same. Jesus gave me a different outlook on life, and I knew from that day He truly completed me. I was done with the "one foot in the world and the other foot in the Lord" life.

And since I made that decision, what a journey it has been! My heart beats only for Him. My life has been forever changed. I'm so thankful for His grace and how He saved me from death so many times. If I would write the stories of God's grace, they'd fill the pages of a hundred books.

It has been two decades since Manuel and I were married. God has blessed us with four beautiful children: Priscilla, Benny, Elijah, and Ariana. We all serve God. We deeply love Him with everything we've got.

My name is Amie Garcia, and I am perfectly broken!

# Chapter 25

# Manuel
## California, USA

*He's the hope that holds me and the Stronghold to shelter me, the only God for me, and my great confidence* (Psalms 91:2 TPT).

I was born and raised in Santa Ana, California. I was the elder son, with a younger sister. I don't remember much except that my father was a hard worker until he was diagnosed with cancer. At six years old, I would go to work the weekends, selling produce on a route we had and at the Nogales High School weekend swap meet in the city of La Puente.

As the cancer metastasized, Father started chemotherapy treatment, which incapacitated him. He could barely function. At just ten years old, I had to drive our car home, all the way from Tustin to Santa Ana—about 5 miles through city traffic.

We prayed for Dad. We would have private services in our home where my Catholic and Presbyterian family members would come and share. I fondly remember those precious times. I remember climbing into his hospital bed as he fought for his life. I have never shared this with anyone. I get teary just thinking about it. I remember saying, "Dad, its ok. Go to sleep. Rest with Jesus." I kissed his forehead and seconds later, he was gone.

My life hit the bottom shortly thereafter. I started skipping school, drinking, doing drugs, and hanging out with the wrong crowd. I joined the gang life; I remember being shot at on almost a nightly basis. I can still see the bullets flying all around me, but none touching me. God's hand was upon me, even though I had walked away from Him.

I moved from Santa Ana to Perris where I met my wife. One day, she invited me to the Presence of the Lord Church where I recommitted my life to Jesus. I had to distance myself from all the negative influences, including some of my family members. I was not going to ever be lured to turn my back on the Lord again.

I continue to count God's blessings today. He has blessed us with four precious children: Priscilla, Benny, Elijah, and Ariana.

My name is Manuel Garcia, and I am perfectly broken.

# Chapter 26

# Timmy
## Cebu, Philippines

*You intended to harm me, but God intended it for good to accomplish what is now being done, the saving of many lives* (Genesis 50:20 NIV).

I live in Cebu, Philippines. I have been blessed with a great wife and three wonderful children. My parents are not perfect by any means, but I think they are the greatest parents in the world. I grew up sheltered, protected, and well-provided. I became a Christian when I was in grade 8, much to the disappointment of my Buddhist family. It took me thirteen years of praying and untiring witnessing to see them come to faith in the Lord Jesus Christ, but it was well worth the wait.

In 2003, the Lord called me into full-time ministry with our church in Makati. My parents, especially Dad, was set against it. But I couldn't be dissuaded. I knew God wanted me to serve Him. Thank God for my wife, who stood with me unwaveringly.

Shortly after I jumped into ministry, I began to see the ugly face of church politics. The squabbles, the underhandedness, and the power struggles within the church leadership were exhausting. I would return home completely wiped out, not so much because of anything important—but because of the infighting. I felt disliked by my superiors. I was seen as insubordinate and unsubmissive because I refused to brownnose them. They expected complete compliance, even when I could clearly see that something was totally wrong.

I remember when my director announced that God had told him to move the church to a specific location next door. We all knew that his motives were wrong, but no one would speak out. When I finally challenged him, I was silenced. As time would show, it wasn't God's will at all. The congregation is still looking for a church home.

Another time, we were raising money for our building just as the senior leader was insisting upon purchasing a brand-new luxury car. When I suggested we downgrade the car and fund his pension plan instead to avoid problematic appearances, I was blacklisted and ultimately transferred to another city with a much smaller startup congregation riddled with issues. I felt so slighted that I almost resigned the pastorate. I considered returning to business. But the Lord instructed me to stay. He said, "Son, whatever they mean for evil, I will turn it around for good." And that is exactly what the Lord has done.

In 2007, I became senior pastor of the Cebu church and currently oversee the entire Visayas region with several churches under my care. What my superior meant for evil, God has indeed turned it around. Most of my peers wonder how we've managed to turn a troubled, contentious congregation into a healthy church family, and we don't have an answer except that we just obeyed God. He is so faithful. To God be the glory!

I am Timmy Lao, and I am perfectly broken.

# Chapter 27

# Jeanne
## California, USA

*No eye has seen, no ear has heard, and no mind has imagined what God has prepared for those who love him*
(1 Corinthians 2:9b).

I grew up in what appeared to be a normal, middle-class American family. I was the third child of five children and my parents raised us as a proper Catholic family. We went to church every Sunday and on all the traditional Christian holidays. What people didn't see was that our family had a huge mask that hid our shame and pain.

My father and mother came from a lot of brokenness, and consequently parented us from these places. My father was very unpredictable in his emotions. He had intense rage, anger, perfectionism, a critical spirit, and prideful judgment that was exacted upon us every day. My older siblings received the brunt of his abuse. As early as I can recall, I was taught unquestioned obedience. Missteps were not tolerated. Dad's need to control fed his selfishness. My mom was very passive, ignoring the harsh realities and pretending life with her husband and children was normal.

At six months old, I almost died from pneumonia. At five, seven, and thirteen years old, I had major surgeries for different ailments. Between ages ten and twelve, I was hospitalized ten times for continuous bouts of pneumonia. I remember being admitted to a major medical center in Los Angeles for cancer testing, along with many other tests, trying to figure out what might be wrong with me. Many of these hospitalizations were very isolating and lonely as my parents had four other children to care for. Eventually at the age of thirteen, I was diagnosed with tuberculosis, scoliosis, and a vascular ring. I was placed on heavy medication for a year, then required to wear a body brace for over a year. Eventually, surgical error paralyzed my vocal cords, which permanently affected my voice projection.

That year also became a huge turning point in my life. My sister's boyfriend, who happened to be ten years older than me, started to seduce me. My dominant father had taught me unquestioned obedience, so I didn't resist his advances. What followed was months of sexual abuse. One day, I gathered the courage to tell my mom, hoping to end the nightmare. To my shock, my parents blamed me for his advances. They thought I had perhaps seduced him and insisted I had to go to the priest to confess my sin. As I sat in that booth, fear, shame, and self-blame filled my soul. The message I was getting was, "Jeanne, you are just not good enough."

When my dad left Mom for another woman, I was confused. On the one hand, I was glad I didn't have to live in fear anymore; but on the other hand, I now felt a fear of abandonment. Life as my family knew it was about to change. Mom's main focus was survival. She never took time to stop and help us heal. Mentally, I froze. I didn't feel like I had permission to dream or think beyond the present. That mindset would remain with me for decades.

One day, at my brother's Bible study, I was introduced to Jesus Christ. I came to know Him not through the lens of religion, but relationship. I found a loving, heavenly Father who didn't judge me, but accepted me unconditionally. Since then, He has used my testimony to bring hope and comfort to many people wherever and whenever I have shared it all around the world.

Today, I am asthma free, healed by the power of God. He has also healed my relationship with Mom and Dad. As I have assumed the primary care for my mother and watched Dad struggle in his latter years, I have experienced God's saving grace. He has unfrozen me, healed my depression, and restored my broken identity.

I continue my adventure with Jesus with radical faith. Dreams I never had as a child, nor would I even dare have, I now boldly dream. Wow…only God could do this.

My name is Jeanne Cameron, and I am perfectly broken

# Chapter 28

# Jesse
## Addis Ababa, Ethiopia

*Being confident of this, that he who began a good work in you will carry it on to completion until the day of Christ Jesus* (Philippians 1:6 NIV).

I used to think that I didn't really have a "testimony," but over the years, I have come to appreciate and draw from my story. It wouldn't be right of me to share my story without sharing about the people who made it possible. I have learned that God is a generational God and the decisions we make affect those who come after us for generations.

My story really begins in Scotland in the year 1873. As my great great grandfather was walking home with a bottle of liquor in his hand, bringing it back for his alcoholic father, he heard an awe-inspiring sound coming from a tent. He went in and immediately was cut to the heart, threw the alcohol away, and ran to the front to get saved. The man who met him at the front was revivalist D. L. Moody. He took a stand that day and decided to live for Jesus. Every generation since then has followed in his footsteps—being "all-in" Christians.

So I grew up under this blessing. I understood that at some point, somebody has to kick the kingdom of darkness to the curb, and say, "No more!" By God's grace, I inherited, not the drunkenness of the Millars, but a redeemed family. And every generation since Grandpa's glorious conversion has gotten closer and closer to Jesus. I've learned that our hard-fought victories of today become tomorrow's normal. Yet, every generation has had to have its own encounter with God's love.

For the majority of my walk with the Lord, I have served Him to earn His favor rather than understanding Him as my Father and me as a son. Deep down even from a young age, I felt unworthy. And I believed the lie that if I wasn't perfect, then I was worthless. I knew so much about the Bible and yet didn't understand the fundamental gospel itself—that it is by grace that we are saved.

Throughout all this, I entered ministry at the very early age of eleven, as the church's assistant janitor. Serving to please I thought. Then at thirteen, God called me as a worship leader in a dramatic encounter with Him. I answered the call. For ten years I led worship sometimes five times a week, during which time I grew in the Lord and in my service to Him. Indeed, I believed in God and served Him, but I still didn't know His love.

One day, I was called upon by a prominent Chinese pastor to join him in leading his church. In a surprising turn of events, the very week I came on staff, he announced his resignation and left me in charge of the Chinese church. Stunned is an understatement, but I stepped up. I was honored to serve Jesus. Over the years, one by one every minority or non-Chinese national was forced out of leadership and I was the last to go. It was a difficult, humiliating season, but I realize now how much I grew and that indeed God had put me there for a reason, both for me and for them.

In 2014, God called my wife and I to the mission field in Ethiopia. As we started making preparations to raise money and move, I was diagnosed with an aggressive case of Lyme disease. My body started deteriorating at an alarming rate. My brain and memory function and nervous system were under attack. All the while, God was drawing me closer to Him. I started having intimacy with Him in ways I never had before. Right in the middle of this catastrophic storm, I started having real peace.

One year after the sickness took hold, I was dramatically healed by the Lord. My wife had helped carry me into the church service that night. I left leaping out of there. The following night, I had one of the deepest most cherished moments with God where I encountered His love. I was no longer afraid, and I have never been the same since. My ministry has never been the same.

Daily, I am learning how to live as one who is loved and serve as such. Indeed, I am still learning, still growing. That is my story.

My name is Jesse Millar, and I am perfectly broken.

# Chapter 29

# Gianna
## California, USA

*In his kindness God called you to share in his eternal glory by means of Christ Jesus. So after you have suffered a little while, he will restore, support, and strengthen you, and he will place you on a firm foundation* (1 Peter 5:10).

I was seventeen years of age when I committed my life to Jesus Christ. Shortly thereafter, I graduated high school; and just as I entered college, everything collapsed. We lost our home.

For more than forty-five days, all six of us were crammed into a small hotel room. All I had to my name were three outfits of clothing to wear. At the same time, I was attending cosmetology school. When my classmates found out about our challenges, the teasing began. My clothes were not always clean. I remember having to expose my smelly socks in pedicure class. I cried every day on my way to school from the hotel.

Eventually, just about all our money was gone. By God's grace, He found us a house. With my cosmetology license in hand, on my way to completing my degree, things seemed to be changing for the better. I started to look for a makeup job.

At that time, I really began seeking the Lord. I yearned for a closer relationship with Him. The relationship with my boyfriend became strained. I felt like he had become an idol, hurting my intimacy with God. "No, God," I protested, "We are having Bible studies, aren't we?" I tried to reason with God. His response, "If you really love him, give him to me." I let him go, along with a few others, leaving me mostly friendless. There I was at twenty years old—no friends, no serious relationship, struggling to make it. I got a job at McDonalds to get myself through college. I tried to enroll in a makeup school in Canada, but the costs were exorbitant.

One day, I met a guy who offered me an internship with his prestigious makeup and special effects studio in North Hollywood. I was told that this experience would be sufficient to secure me a career without needing a degree. Surprisingly, my job didn't seem to have much to do with makeup. I was cleaning toilets, baseboards, mopping floors, doing laundry, and other menial chores. I felt invisible. They kept telling me, "Just work for me for free here and eventually you will be picked up. You're gonna do this; you're gonna be big, you're gonna be great!" It seemed as though everyone else was making it except me.

I decided it was time to move on. I left and took on full-time hours at McDonalds. Friends would say, "Wow, Gianna…you're working here with a cosmetology license?" I would work there for another two years before God moved me on, but I carried failure with me.

Dr. Dennis said something to me one day, "Gianna, you can be more and have more." That simple statement jolted me. I realized that I had camped out in my wilderness. I had so many insecurities, self-doubt, jealousy, pride, and self-hatred. I hated being black. I hated my hair. I hated every part of who God made me.

By His grace, God tore down every one of those lies. I found my identity in Him. He healed me of this distorted view of myself. I would be who He made me to be. I would wear my hair proudly, naturally if need be, without shame. God set me free.

My heart is not the same. I am not the same broken girl trying to make it. I enjoy styling hair and applying makeup now because I enjoy helping others. I'm happy. I know who I am now, so how could I not be successful? In a nutshell, God broke my dependency on others and redirected my eyes to always be on Him.

My name is Gianna Greer, and I am perfectly broken!

# Chapter 30

# Duncan
## Kampala, Uganda

*Though he was God, he did not think of equality with God as something to cling to. Instead, he gave up his divine privileges; he took the humble position of a slave and was born as a human being. When he appeared in human form* (Philippians 2:6-7).

I was raised as a devout Anglican. My big brother, Dr. Dennis Sempebwa, had already accepted Jesus Christ as his Lord and Savior. He is the firstborn in our family. I remember how he used to seek God. He became actively involved in ministry in a couple of churches around the city. It is at one of those churches that I realized my need for Christ, even though my devotion to religion had protected me from some common youthful indulgences. I was fourteen years of age.

One year later, I had a terrible accident. I tripped and fell down several flights of stairs, hitting my head on the concrete. I blacked out. I was rushed to Mulago Hospital, which was the top government hospital with access to the top doctors in the nation, including Uganda's best neurosurgeon who told my parents, "We have to operate on him or he dies."

The next morning, the doctor announced, "The place has healed. In all the years that I have practiced medicine, I have never seen anything like this." God had supernaturally intervened.

Jesus kept me out of trouble—away from alcohol, premarital sex, and all the things that many people my age were doing—much to the irritation of my schoolmates.

Despite my devout lifestyle, I still felt empty inside. Life at home was rough. My dad used to drink alcohol a lot. He became prominent and started making a lot of money working for the United Nations Industrial Development Organization. He traveled a lot. Along with his job came a certain lifestyle that included cars, alcohol, women, and so on. All that pushed me to seek for real answers in my newfound faith. That quest led me to embrace Christ as the answer to my broken life.

Indeed, God has been amazing. I believe that if He had not saved me, I would not be alive. And, even if I had survived that accident, my life would be totally different from what it is now. All my life, everything I have, revolves around Jesus as my Lord and Savior. My worldview is different, everything has changed, because of Him.

I am thankful for Dr. Dennis and his faith in God. He has inspired me, and indeed our whole family, to love and serve Jesus Christ.

I am still on a journey. My story is still being written. My walk with Christ has not been without obstacles and storms. The temptation for self-pity has been significant. Why should we suffer if we know Jesus? Unfortunately, the teachers in my life were echoing the same pessimistic ideology or theology. Thank God He has taught me that although Christians suffer as others do—we have a hope in Christ.

Jesus has totally changed my life—the way I think, the way I look at everything in life—and I am grateful for that. I am thankful to God for where He has brought me, where He is taking me.

My name is Duncan Sempebwa, and I am perfectly broken.

# Chapter 31

# Lisa
## California, USA

*Create in me a pure heart, O God, and renew a steadfast spirit within me. Do not cast me from your presence or take your Holy Spirit from me. Restore to me the joy of your salvation and grant me a willing spirit, to sustain me* (Psalms 51:10-12 NIV).

A friend and I decided to attend a sports event at our high school one night. Since we were running late, we decided to take a shortcut through a deserted parking lot. Suddenly, a van pulled up and out of nowhere, a gang of guys jumped out and forced us in. Yes, we were abducted—and what followed would forever shape our lives.

For hours we were tortured and gang raped. I remember the van door opening and shutting as one by one each of them violated us throughout the long night. The shackles left me helpless, confused, and disoriented. The pain was indescribable. Soon, the lights and sounds faded away as I passed out.

The next thing I remember was daylight and the feeling of grass. I realized I was in a field alone. They had used us, dumped us, and left us for dead. I felt pain, fear, and immense brokenness. *What happened? Where's my friend? Why am I here? How did I even get here?* Then I lost consciousness again.

When I opened my eyes, I was in a hospital. The questions returned. *Why am I here?* Evidently, the police who found me knew my father, otherwise I would have been a Jane Doe. As I forced my eyes to open, I saw my precious family and faintly heard the doctor's prognosis.

"She is completely torn up inside. We will do whatever we can to help her, but just so you know, she will never be able to bear children."

Ten days later, I was discharged. I was in physical and emotional pain. Prior to that night, I was a virgin; a good girl. Stuff like that only happened to bad girls, not me. We were a good family. All my ideals were shuttered. I could see my family grappling with the reality of my abduction. Understandably, they struggled with it. They refused to come to terms with the randomness of the incident. "Maybe a boyfriend did this?" "What if she seduced them and things got out of hand." The questions, the empty stares drove me into isolation. The pain was unbearable.

Finally, I decided they didn't care for me. I needed to get out of there; and at age fifteen, I ran away from my childhood home. *I will make a life for myself,* I thought. *I don't need them. I don't need anybody!*

That started a long struggle with inner pain. Voices of rejection and guilt screamed inside my head. At fifteen, I had to get a job to support myself. I dropped out of school and escaped further to drug abuse. Somehow, drugs seemed to be able to mask my deep pain. For the next few years, I would jump from one abusive relationship to the next.

I finally found a man, got married, and settled down for a while. In spite of the dire medical prognosis, I became pregnant with Cassandra. She was everything to me. Unfortunately, I would realize that I was one of several women in my husband's life. That devastated me, and consequently, drove me back into a life of drug abuse. I felt myself slipping away, unable to mask the pain. I started to lose everything I considered valuable—job, home, friends, and eventually, Cassandra, the one person I loved more than anything. I knew I needed help, but felt completely helpless. I was living on the streets, completely abandoned with nowhere to turn.

One day a guy was hiring help for his construction business. He hired me, which infuriated my abusive boyfriend who had just taken me in for a few nights off the streets. He was using me in exchange for drugs. When I returned from work that first morning, he picked me up and slammed me against a wall while spewing vile threats. Miraculously, I freed myself and ran back to my new boss, Dean. "Please help me,"

I pleaded as I banged on the door. He gave me a clear choice—continue down the path I was going or come travel with him. I chose the latter and that one decision changed the entire trajectory of my life.

Dean introduced me to a friend who talked a lot about Jesus. *Jesus… where has He been all these years while I suffered?* I asked myself. Because of the grip of drug addiction, nightmares, and emotional torment, I was at my wit's end. Something had to give. I needed an intervention. One night, I angrily pointed to the heavens and cried out, "Jesus, if You are who You say You are, and if You love me like they tell me You love me, then You need to show up now, because I am broken, I am weak, and I cannot do this without You. I surrender. And if You rescue me, I will serve You all the days of my life." And I passed out.

The next morning, I woke up completely free. Even my countenance had changed. I felt no urge to do drugs, and haven't to this very day, decades later. The Lord transformed my life and at that point started my journey of service to Him. Dean and I were married, raised a family, built a successful business, and continue to touch nations with Christ's love.

My name is Lisa Romesburg, and I am perfectly broken.

# Chapter 32

# Ingrid
## Texas, USA

*I can never escape from your Spirit! I can never get away from your presence! If I go up to heaven, you are there; if I go down to the grave, you are there. If I ride the wings of the morning, if I dwell by the farthest oceans, even there your hand will guide me, and your strength will support me. I could ask the darkness to hide me and the light around me to become night—but even in darkness I cannot hide from you. To you the night shines as bright as day. Darkness and light are the same to you* (Psalms 139:7-12).

I was born in Bucharest, Romania, in 1974. At the time, the country was in despair since it had been in the hands of a Stalinist, Marxist one-party government and a new president, a dictator, had just been elected who was preparing to turn the country into a totalitarian dictatorship. Food, gasoline, and other necessities were thinly dispersed.

My parents were incurable dreamers and very adventurous by nature. My father navigated ships for the commercial navy, and my mother had quit her job to care for my brother and I when I was born. She had to share a bed with another woman in labor while birthing me. Hospitals were very unsanitary and overpopulated. Everyone was hungry, over-worked, and constantly looking for ways to survive. We were like animals in a cage, starved and secluded from the world.

When the communists took power, they appointed themselves positions of power and established a new political system. They very quickly confiscated all guns and redistributed the wealth of the rich to the poor of the country. Unfortunately, the poor didn't know how to run, maintain, or make profits so the farms and businesses failed. Thus, the economic condition of the country degenerated. My grandmother lived through this time.

The communists assigned labels to the population census such as "origina sanatoasa" meaning "healthy social origin" for the new top tier, meaning the new owners of the distributed wealth. And conversely assigned "origina ne-sanatoasa," meaning "unhealthy social origin," to the new lower class. One had to have a "healthy social origin" status in order to be able to have any access to education or a decent job. So the population that was lower class was now considered upper class, labeled as such on the National Census, and given benefits no longer available to the original upper class.

My family was labeled "unhealthy social origin" because both of my grandparents were well-to-do. They had owned large plots of land, the general store, and had laid out the streets of their town. After that, it was very difficult for us to work toward owning anything and provide for our families. Food was rationed; and when we ran out of ration tickets, we were not permitted to purchase any more. Even when we had tickets, we were sometimes denied food because we were of the "unhealthy social origin."

The routine was the same—as soon as we heard there was a food supply truck on its way to our neighborhood, we would line up at the main entrance to buy meager rations before they ran out. I remember going with my grandfather to wait in line. We would wait all day, sitting on crates and talking with neighbors. At night, my mother would come to relieve my grandfather and I would stay in line all night with her until the next afternoon when the truck arrived. I can still see the struggle to unload the truck because there were so many people trying to push through. I remember my mom as she ran arms straight in front of her trying to get through to the front of the line.

We never knew when the next truck was coming and how much it had to deliver. Lunch was often a slice of bread and butter. My grandparents raised chickens, pigs, and nutria for meat and fur. People killed and ate any animal in sight…I remember seeing friends chase a rabbit for food.

There were fruit and nut trees we ate from. I sometimes helped my grandfather crush the grapes for wine with my feet. We all had gardens with vegetables and herbs, which we watered with rain water. We also had a bakery that produced bread daily. That was a lifesaver. I had never seen hot dogs or bananas until my dad brought some home from a trip abroad. We made do like everyone else. We were privileged enough to have a four-seater Dacia car that would fit all six of us in it. Every room in our apartment had a bed in it so that everyone could sleep on a bed.

At the time, being in the military meant mandatory membership in the communist party, but my father was an outspoken opponent, and soon it became clear to his superiors that he would be a negative influence. You see, every time he docked a commercial navy ship abroad, they ran the risk of him defecting, so they had the rest of us family members at home carefully watched.

It was nearly impossible to leave the country without approval from the government. My father could leave because he was navigating the ships for trade. He would come home and tell us stories of how people lived in other countries—they were not waiting in line for food nor fearing for their lives. He and Mom discussed defection but that would leave us very exposed to retaliation, not to mention him being caught and killed.

When my youngest brother was born, it became clear that we couldn't afford to make it on such meager resources. We had to apply to leave the country legally. Merely filing the petition to emigrate was dangerous. Dad kept filing petitions until they got fed up with him and asked him to report to the local office for questioning. This was scary as many people went "missing" after such questioning. My parents enlisted the help of a doctor friend who admitted him into a hospital for "treatment." They never asked to question him again.

The typical waiting time for approval was five to seven years. Some even waited ten years. My father continued to work in the commercial navy, and we kept to our everyday lives, trying not to draw any attention to ourselves. Even so, we were followed everywhere we went. Whenever Dad was deployed, there was often an officer in uniform standing under our balcony in the honeysuckle bush and one at our front door. My father was also followed on the ship. The idea was to keep us afraid that something would happen to one of us if we got out of line or if Dad defected.

Mom went to work while we went to school. We didn't want to raise any alarms; but unfortunately, word got out that we were trying to leave the country and the school revoked my accolades. We had our church family, most of whom were in the same boat as we were—waiting to receive approval to leave. Generally, Christians were considered trouble-makers because many would not join the communist party. Problem is, you could not opt out. In fact, the national ID card indicated that the holder was a member of the communist party.

During that time, I was touched by the plight of the gypsy children in a town farther into the countryside. I expressed to my mom that we couldn't let them go hungry and she got all her friends to cash in their food ration cards. They donated half their food and we took time during the weekends to deliver the food to the gypsy kids. My heart was branded with compassion for children in need. I will never forget how hungry they were. Some were beaten by their parents but had snuck out of the house to come get a little food. I think I was five or six years old. For the first time I saw hunger, pain, fear, hopelessness—and I also saw joy, wonder, relief, and thankfulness. Those visits changed my life forever.

One night, I had a dream that our family was approved to leave the country. In the morning, I told my mother and she replied with an "Amen," affirming her approval. Three days later, we received our notices to emigrate, something unheard of for new applicants like us.

My parents began to sell our possessions to try and raise funds for our airfares. One day, someone approached my father about buying our car and offered him the exact amount we needed to purchase our airline tickets! Miracles abounded and we counted the days until our departure. Before leaving, we would have to surrender all our possessions to the government and submit our luggage for inspection several days before departure.

The night before leaving, we slept, dressed, at my grandmother's apartment. I could imagine that is how the Israelites felt before leaving Egypt. We had to be very quiet. The chances of someone reporting us to the local authorities was very real. Morning came, and we were rushed to the airport. I remember the formalities of checking papers and staying together. I remember being in my seat on the flight, buckled in and ready to go. Then I remember the plane being stopped while taxiing and my father being called off the plane. I looked over through the window and saw all our luggage—six large green army sacks—lined up on the tarmac.

The phony complaint was that we had not paid our luggage tax. Dad was to either pay the tax, which we had already paid, or leave the luggage and reboard the flight. My father decided on the spot to leave our luggage behind. Some of our friends had given us some Romanian cultural dolls and had hidden 20 American dollars in one of the doll's clothes. Carrying US dollars was illegal and punishable by imprisonment. We did not know that when Dad decided to leave the luggage behind. However, when we landed in Italy, we realized that three of our bags had been reloaded and had arrived with us. In that luggage, we found the dolls and money. We were so thankful as we didn't have any money with us.

We spent eight days in an Italian Refugee Camp while awaiting out visa issuance. We slept in a giant room with bunk beds and some on cement floors, but they served us amazing meals. My older brother got a job as a messenger in order to make some money for the family. We didn't know how long we were going to be there.

By God's grace, a church in Chicago sponsored us and they paid for our tickets to fly out of Italy and into the United States. Our asylum application was granted, and soon we were on our way to the USA. I will never forget my father dropping to his knees and kissing the ground at the end of the jetway at New York's JFK Airport.

We were dirty and tired, but we still had a connecting flight to Chicago. Church members from our church in Romania picked us up at the airport. They took us to an apartment where we would stay for the duration of our transition. They filled our refrigerator with food that we had never seen before. They helped enroll us in school and offered my father various janitorial jobs. In the evenings, we patrolled the streets collecting cans for recycling to earn some money to subsist. Saturdays we spent hours with Dad at the junkyard looking for car parts. Life was hard, but wonderful. No one followed or persecuted us.

Food was around every corner and we knew there was no limit to what we could strive for.

I am so thankful for my parents who took such risks so that we can have the freedom the USA offers; and though my heart was born in Bucharest, it belongs to the United States. My growing-up experience feels like a dream now with dangers and escapes as seen in action movies, but the Lord carried us through. While many were killed or died from hopelessness, we thank God for His grace to sing of His providence and mercy.

My name is Ingrid Sempebwa, and I am perfectly broken.

# Chapter 33

# Dennis
## Texas, USA

*But those who trust in the LORD will find new strength.
They will soar high on wings like eagles. They will run and
not grow weary. They will walk and not faint* (Isaiah 40:31).

I was born and raised in Uganda, East Africa. It was the thirteenth poorest country in the world at that time, so poverty, lack, and diseases were my lot. During wartime, we would sometimes look for mangos or guavas on trees in hopes of finding something to eat for lunch. Essentials like shoes and bookbags were luxuries. Having had an absent, philandering father, my mother was left to carry the load.

To make matters worse, there was political anarchy. The rule of law was virtually nonexistent. It was common for bands of underpaid army cohorts to pillage a village, raping every female—ranging in age from three to eighty—while indiscriminately murdering anyone else they deemed a threat. I vividly remember jumping over dead bodies of fallen fellow citizens on my way to school. I also remember hiding in bushes as I heard neighbors pleading for their lives and dignity at the hands of drunken military police. And I remember the countless funerals of schoolmates who had been slaughtered or shot by renegade military platoons.

Life seemed to be telling me, "Dennis, you will never become anything at all. If you don't die by the bullet, something else will take you out. Like your predecessors, you will die—you'll become a dead-beat dad, a womanizer, and an alcoholic."

One day, Mom announced, "Dennis, you and me are going to a crusade tomorrow."

"Crusade, what's that?" I asked.

"You'll see!" she said.

It really didn't matter what it was we were going to do. I just wanted to get out of the house and go to the big city, Kampala, with my mother.

That day there were thousands of people gathered at the city square. All of a sudden, a flamboyantly dressed man jumped up and introduced himself to the crowd. "My name is Dr. Benson Idahosa and I have been sent here by God from Nigeria to preach Jesus to you." So I'm thinking, *What is this all about? Jesus is more of a historical figure, but this guy seems to be talking to Him like He is right here. What's that all about?*

Just then, Dr. Idahosa said, "No, He is not some historical figure. Jesus is alive and well and He wants to come into your life!"

Now I'm thinking, *That's freaky. How on earth can God come into a human life?* Almost right away, Dr. Idahosa said, "He comes into your life by living His life within you."

Then I thought, *If He is really real, one thing I would really want from Him is peace. I want all this fear gone out of my life.* In almost direct response to my mental inquiry, Dr. Idahosa roars, "Uganda is in turmoil, but only Jesus can give you true peace. You see, the peace of God passes all understanding." I was totally freaked out.

Then I thought, *Ok, I want this.* My understanding was pretty pathetic. My mind was telling me that I would never grow up and that I was going to die—but if God's peace could bypass or surpass my understanding, I wanted it! Almost immediately, Dr. Idahosa invited those gathered to accept Christ. I ran right up to the front with my precious mother. We both accepted Christ that day.

While we were walking home after the meeting, I was kind of disappointed that "nothing" had happened. I expected something dramatic to happen to me, like maybe I should have gotten zapped with His peace, right? But I noticed a strange calm about me. Typically, evenings were filled with terror. I was always terrified of the night. *Would there be a military raid tonight? What if my sisters got raped by soldiers patrolling the streets?* Strangely, none of those nightly thoughts bothered me. When we returned home that evening, the guys asked,

"Dennis, what's wrong?" All I could say was, "I don't know...Jesus!" I didn't have a theological explanation for what had happened to me. All I knew was I accepted Jesus.

The next morning I woke up smiling, grateful that the calmness hadn't worn off. I happily walked to school, excited to share my peace with all my friends. Mornings were typically somber—it's when we counted who was missing, which meant that they were probably dead or their families had been displaced during the night. "What's wrong with you?" my friends asked. "Why the smile?"

I said, "I don't know, I'm just happy...Jesus." They were curious. Over the next month, I led scores of them to the lovingkindness of Jesus Christ.

Interestingly, the world around me didn't change much. In fact, it got worse as military coup after military coup ensued and external peace continued to elude our country for years. But Jesus became our peace and has continued to be throughout the past four decades.

Today, I get to travel the nations and share His incredible story. To God be the glory!

My name is Dennis Sempebwa, and I am perfectly broken.

# Conclusion

A few days after I accepted Christ, I volunteered to join the street evangelism team. I figured I had to share what God had done for me. Problem is, I didn't know what evangelism was or how to do it.

To share Christ with the community, every afternoon the street evangelism team would set up a small platform right in the middle of the busiest street market in the city. They would sing a couple of songs, and then one by one, believers would share their testimonies.

It was a hot afternoon when I first volunteered to share my story. I was nervous. "I was a thief!" cried Brother John. "I terrorized my village, stealing every goat I could find. Then Jesus came into my life and now I am saved!" The crowd roared with claps of affirmation and rejoicing. Then came the next brother with pretty much the same kind of testimony. In fact, his was even more colorful. Then it hits me—I didn't really have a story. What was I going to share. At twelve years old, I was the youngest member of the team.

Sister Rhoda announced, "Next, we have a young man who just received Jesus. He will now share his testimony." Right as I took the bull horn to share, one of the men in the audience said, "Well, tell us what you did before Jesus changed you." I froze. I stammered through a disjointed testimony about God saving little children too. With a handful of claps, I walked off the makeshift stage, mortified.

"Well done, Dennis," encouraged Brother John. "Let's do this again tomorrow." No way was I ever going to do that again. I told him that I really had no testimony, so I would not be participating again. I am thankful that Brother John didn't allow me to quit. He taught me to never judge experiences or compare stories. Everyone has a path that is unique to each of us.

I hope you've been blessed by these different stories. Some are short, while others are long or more dramatic. Regardless, they are all God's stories. It is my hope that each testimony has encouraged you to trust Him with the broken pieces of your life—knowing now that He is with you every step of the way, making you whole and wholly loved.

# About the Author

Dennis Sempebwa was born in Uganda, Africa. He is the founder and president of Eagle's Wings International (EWI), a global missionary organization with hubs in twenty-five countries. EWI reaches tens of millions of thirsty people with the unadulterated gospel of our Lord Jesus Christ.

Dr. Sempebwa also serves as the president and CEO of The Sahara Wisdom Center, a multinational training corporation committed to inspiring transformational thinking in academia, entertainment, business, and government institutions in developing countries.

Dr. Sempebwa has served in more than seventy countries and authored more than a dozen books. He is a global goodwill ambassador and a highly sought-after speaker who holds numerous graduate and postgraduate degrees.

Dr. Sempebwa has been married to his beloved wife, Ingrid, for twenty-three years. They are blessed with five children: Adam, Abigail, Caleb, Judah, and Elijah. They currently reside in North Texas in the United States.

Dr. Dennis Sempebwa may be contacted at: e-wings.net; swc.life; Facebook, Twitter, and Instagram.

# Other Books by Dr. Dennis D. Sempebwa

- Entourage
- Surrounding Yourself with the Right People
- The Substance of Things Hoped For
- Timeless Truths
- Deadly Distractions
- You Have a Dream

Publishing Services by
EVANGELISTA MEDIA & CONSULTING

Via Maiella, 1
66020 San Giovanni Teatino (CH) – Italy

publisher@evangelistamedia.com

www.evangelistamedia.com

/evangelistamediaconsulting

evangelista_media_consulting

Made in the USA
San Bernardino, CA
29 November 2019